Economic Effects
of Social Security

Studies of Government Finance: Second Series

TITLES PUBLISHED

Economic Effects
of Social Security

HENRY J. AARON

Studies of Government Finance

THE BROOKINGS INSTITUTION

WASHINGTON, D.C.

58,090

THE BROOKINGS INSTITUTION is an independent organization devoted to nonpartisan research, education, and publication in economics, government, foreign policy, and the social sciences generally. Its principal purposes are to aid in the development of sound public policies and to promote public understanding of issues of national importance.

The Institution was founded on December 8, 1927, to merge the activities of the Institute for Government Research, founded in 1916, the Institute of Economics, founded in 1922, and the Robert Brookings Graduate School of Economics and Government, founded in 1924.

The Board of Trustees is responsible for the general administration of the Institution, while the immediate direction of the policies, program, and staff is vested in the President, assisted by an advisory committee of the officers and staff. The by-laws of the Institution state: "It is the function of the Trustees to make possible the conduct of scientific research, and publication, under the most favorable conditions, and to safeguard the independence of the research staff in the pursuit of their studies and in the publication of the results of such studies. It is not a part of their function to determine, control, or influence the conduct of particular investigations or the conclusions reached."

The President bears final responsibility for the decision to publish a manuscript as a Brookings book. In reaching his judgment on the competence, accuracy, and objectivity of each study, the President is advised by the director of the appropriate research program and weighs the views of a panel of expert outside readers who report to him in confidence on the quality of the work. Publication of a work signifies that it is deemed a competent treatment worthy of public consideration but does not imply endorsement of conclusions or recommendations.

The Institution maintains its position of neutrality on issues of public policy in order to safeguard the intellectual freedom of the staff. Hence interpretations or conclusions in Brookings publications should be understood to be solely those of the authors and should not be attributed to the Institution, to its trustees, officers, or other staff members, or to the organizations that support its research.

For my son, Jeffrey

Foreword

THE SOCIAL SECURITY SYSTEM—the largest government domestic program in the United States and an important source of retirement income for a large number of Americans—began to suffer from serious financial problems during the mid-1970s. At first, the deficits reflected the sharp slowdown in current economic growth. But even larger deficits were projected for the twenty-first century under the impact of declining birthrates and an aging population.

For these and other reasons, economists undertook theoretical and empirical work to measure the economic effects of the social security system. The result was an outpouring of analyses, increasingly technical and inaccessible to lay observers, but increasingly important to them because of the decisions that will have to be made affecting their taxes and retirement benefits.

In May 1981 President Reagan proposed a number of reductions in social security benefits. In response to the hostile reception his proposals received, the president created a bipartisan National Commission on Social Security Reform. The issues to be addressed by the commission will be on the public agenda for many years.

As the nation turns to the important decisions on social security that lie ahead, it is important that members of Congress, the press, and the public understand the influence of social security on saving, labor supply, and the distribution of income. The book is intended to contribute to that understanding. It is another in a series of Brookings books that reflect the Institution's continuing concern with the adequacy and financial soundness of the social security system. They include *Social Security: Perspectives for Reform*, by Joseph A. Pechman, Henry J. Aaron, and Michael K. Taussig (1968); *The Payroll Tax for Social Security*, by John A. Brittain (1972); *The Future of Social Security*, by Alicia H. Munnell (1977); and *Policymaking for Social Security*, by Martha Derthick (1979).

Henry J. Aaron is a senior fellow in the Brookings Economic Studies

ix

program and professor of economics at the University of Maryland. He is grateful for the comments of Robert M. Ball, Alan S. Blinder, Gary T. Burtless, Harvey Galper, Dean R. Leimer, Selig D. Lesnoy, Robert A. Moffitt, Robert J. Myers, Joseph A. Pechman, and Lawrence Thompson. Diane E. Levin and Lisa James provided research assistance. The manuscript was edited by Karen J. Wirt; its factual content was verified by Penelope S. Harpold. The project was supported by a grant from the U.S. Department of Health and Human Services for research on retirement income policy. This book is the sixteenth in the second series of Brookings Studies in Government Finance.

The views expressed here are the author's alone and should not be ascribed to the Department of Health and Human Services, or to the trustees, officers, or other staff members of the Brookings Institution or the University of Maryland.

BRUCE K. MAC LAURY
President

September 1982
Washington, D.C.

Contents

Table

Figures

CHAPTER ONE

Introduction

RESEARCH on how social security influences personal saving, labor supply, and the distribution of income has become a major growth industry among economists in the United States. The reasons are obvious.

Social security is the largest nondefense governmental program in the United States; cash payments constituted 6.8 percent of personal disposable income in 1981, and estimates of the present discounted value of present and future social security entitlements rose from 1.8 trillion to 3.6 trillion 1972 dollars in 1977, depending on the method of estimation.[1] Entitlements to future social security benefits are the most important asset of most American families, and actual benefits have played a central part in reducing poverty among the aged. At the same time, economic performance in the United States has deteriorated in the past decade. Increased work effort and investment would boost aggregate output.[2]

Several economists have presented theoretical and empirical evidence in support of the contention that the growth of social security and specific characteristics of the system have contributed to that poor economic performance by reducing both labor supply and savings. Other econo-

1. These estimates are taken from Dean R. Leimer and Selig D. Lesnoy, "Social Security and Private Saving: New Time-Series Evidence," *Journal of Political Economy*, vol. 90 (June 1982), pp. 606–29. These estimates of social security wealth are explained below. They exclude health and disability benefits; including them would drastically increase the estimates because the cost of health insurance is projected to rise dramatically in future years. See *1982 Annual Report, Federal Old Age and Survivors Insurance and Disability Insurance Trust Funds*, H. Doc. 97-163, 97 Cong. 2 sess. (Government Printing Office, 1982).

2. Whether they would increase economic welfare, including the value of leisure, is open to academic challenge. As shown in the next chapter, labor force participation is at an all-time high in the United States. But unemployment is also at postwar highs. See William Nordhaus and James Tobin, "Is Growth Obsolete?" *Economic Research: Retrospect and Prospect*, vol. 5, *Proceedings of the Fiftieth Anniversary Colloquium on Economic Growth* (Columbia University Press for the National Bureau of Economic Research, 1972).

1

mists have challenged almost every one of these arguments. In fact, reputable economists may be found who argue that social security has decreased savings, increased savings, or had no perceptible effect. Similarly, economists may be found who hold that social security has increased labor supply, reduced it, left it unchanged, or caused offsetting changes in labor supply by workers of different ages.

It is safe to say that at this time no major issue concerning the effect of social security on economic behavior has been settled to the satisfaction of a dominant majority of analysts. In view of its size, however, it would be surprising if social security did not change economic behavior. So analysts will keep trying to pin down those effects.

In the meantime, however, policymakers must make decisions on social security, even if analysts cannot agree. The natural and proper reaction of decisionmakers to the disarray among analysts will be to increase the weight they attach to their perceptions of equity, adequacy of benefits, fairness of taxes, and similar qualitative considerations. Nevertheless, lay observers can try to understand how analysts go about their work and why they are so uncertain. This book is intended to help them do just that.

The Social Security Program

Congress enacted the Social Security Act in 1935. Payroll taxes were first collected in 1937, and the first monthly benefits were paid in 1940.[3] In 1939 Congress took a number of decisions that slowed the buildup of reserves; and because benefits grew slowly (reaching only $961 million by 1950), taxes also remained modest. Not until 1950 did taxes equal 1 percent of personal income (see figure 1). Only 60 percent of the labor force was covered until the early 1950s when Congress made eligibility almost universal.[4]

3. Lump-sum payments to families of workers who had died and to those reaching age sixty-five were paid before 1940.
4. Permanent federal civilian employees and some state and local employees, about 10 percent of the labor force, remain without social security coverage, but nearly all other workers have coverage. Furthermore, most people working in jobs without coverage at a particular time earn rights to benefits from work with coverage at some time during their working lives. As a result, by the year 2000 an estimated 97 percent of all workers will be eligible for benefits when they reach retirement age. See Robert M. Ball, *Social Security Today and Tomorrow* (Columbia University Press, 1978), p. 108.

Figure 1. *Old Age and Survivors Disability Insurance Benefits, Taxes, and Reserves as a Percent of Personal Income, 1937–80*

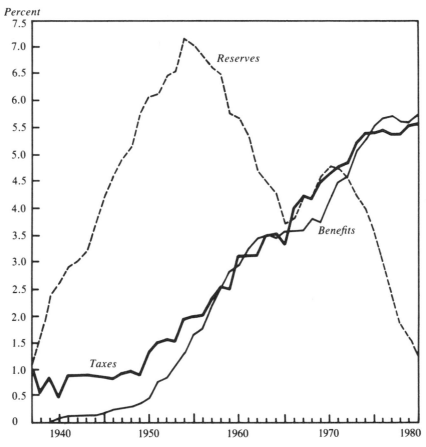

Source: Social Security Administration, *Social Security Bulletin, Annual Statistical Supplement, 1980* (Government Printing Office, 1980), pp. 83–85, 105.

At various times Congress has added to the list of contingencies under which benefits are paid. The Social Security Act initially covered retirees at age sixty-five and provided a lump-sum death benefit. Even before the first benefit checks were written, Congress in 1939 broadened the list of potential beneficiaries to include widows, surviving parents and children of deceased workers, and the wives and children of retirees (husbands and widowers were added in 1950). In 1956 Congress added benefits for disabled workers and provided that women aged sixty-two to sixty-four could claim reduced retirement benefits; the right to claim retirement benefits at age sixty-two was extended to men in 1961.[5]

In brief, social security now pays cash benefits in three situations. When workers reach age sixty-two and have worked for just under eight years in employment with social security coverage, they are eligible to receive retirement benefits, and extra benefits are paid to spouses and to dependent children.[6] The benefits are based on average earnings over an extended period—twenty-six years for those turning sixty-two in 1982.[7] If beneficiaries continue to work past age sixty-two, benefits are increased by $8\frac{1}{3}$ percent for the first three years and by smaller percentages in succeeding years.[8] Benefits are also paid to workers with social security coverage who become disabled and to their spouses and dependent children. Disability is defined on the basis of physical impairments, age, education, and other personal factors that prevent workers from performing any substantial gainful activity. Disability is judged to have ended if, upon reexamination, a person is found not to be suffering from any such condition or if that person demonstrates the ability to engage in substantial gainful activity by earning more than a specified

5. Martha Derthick, *Policymaking for Social Security* (Brookings Institution, 1979), pp. 429–32.

6. Eventually a ten-year work history will be required for eligibility.

7. Even if workers have fewer than twenty-six years in covered employment, earnings consist only of those received in covered employment; earnings in other jobs are disregarded. The number of years used in computing benefit rises by one year for each calendar year until the total number of included years reaches thirty-five.

8. The adjustment is described as a $6\frac{2}{3}$ percent reduction for each year a worker retires before age sixty-five and a 3 percent bonus for each year the worker remains on the job after age sixty-five up to age seventy-two. In practice, the adjustment is done on the basis of each month in which benefits are reduced because earnings have exceeded an allowable maximum. The adjustment is $\frac{5}{9}$ percent per month of the benefit payable at age sixty-five or, equivalently, $\frac{25}{36}$ percent of the benefit payable at age sixty-two.

The straightforward way of putting the adjustment is that a worker is eligible to receive benefits at age sixty-two and receives a bonus of $8\frac{1}{3}$ percent of the age sixty-two benefit for each of the next three years of work and $3\frac{3}{4}$ percent of the age sixty-two benefit for each of the next seven years of work. This increase takes account of the fact that because older claimants are likely to receive benefits for a shorter time than younger ones, the system can afford to pay more to workers whose benefits are deferred because of current earnings. For workers between ages sixty-two and sixty-five, the adjustment is almost fully "actuarial" in the sense that the expected value of benefits for the average worker is substantially unaffected by whether benefits are deferred or not. For workers between ages sixty-five and seventy-two, the adjustment is less than actuarial in the sense that deferral of benefits because of current earnings reduces the long-run expected cost of benefit payments. Beneficiaries who are age seventy-two or older are not subject to the earnings test.

amount (now $300 per month) for more than nine months. Finally, cash benefits are paid to the surviving spouse and dependent children of workers who die. In December 1981 the average newly awarded retirement and disability benefits were $396 and $430 per month, respectively. By comparison, the average wage of workers in private nonagricultural employment in 1981 was $1,094 per month.[9]

Differences between Annuities and Social Security

Even this incomplete summary of present law and its history makes clear the inappropriateness of treating social security as a simple annuity payable at a certain age after payment of "tax-premiums" for a number of years. In fact, social security is an amalgam of five key sets of features, each of which is involved in the determination of the economic effects of the system as a whole.

First, the social security benefit formula is a progressive function of average wages earned in covered employment over most of each eligible person's working life.[10] That is, the ratio of benefits to average earnings is higher for workers with low average earnings than for those with high average earnings. Because the payroll tax used to finance social security benefits is proportional to covered earnings up to the earnings ceiling ($32,400 in 1982),[11] the ratio of benefits to the accumulated value of taxes paid is higher for workers with low earnings than for those with high earnings. While economists at various times have debated the incidence of the payroll tax, the preponderance of professional opinion holds that workers bear the burden of the payroll tax, whether it is legally imposed on the workers themselves or their employers.[12] To the extent that the

9. This amount is based on the average weekly wage reported in the *1982 Economic Report of the President, February 1982*, table B-39, p. 277.

10. The average wage used in computing benefits for workers reaching age sixty-two in 1982 usually is based on the twenty-seven years of highest indexed covered earnings after 1950. The number of years in the averaging period rises by one with each passing year until 1991 after which benefits will be based on the highest thirty-five years of covered earnings.

11. The payroll tax is levied in 1982 at a rate of 6.7 percent on both employees and employers; self-employed workers pay tax at a rate of 9.35 percent. Both rates are scheduled under present law to increase in 1985 to 7.05 percent and 9.9 percent, respectively.

12. John A. Brittain, *The Payroll Tax for Social Security* (Brookings Institution, 1972), finds that the payroll tax is borne by labor. Martin S. Feldstein, "Tax Incidence in a Growing Economy with Variable Factor Supply," *Quarterly Journal of Economics*, vol.

tax is simply prepayment for later benefits, payroll taxes and entitlements offset one another and there is no burden to allocate.

The second important feature of the social security system is that the difference between the expected value of benefits and the accumulated value of taxes paid is now large and has nearly peaked.[13] Workers who received benefits in 1940 and who could have paid taxes for no more than four years received a very high implicit rate of return on those taxes. Later cohorts of workers have faced higher rates of tax and paid them for more years. For all cohorts of workers who have reached age sixty-two thus far, the rate of return on taxes paid—taking account of the various kinds of benefits payable under the social security system—has far exceeded the rate of return generally available on marketable assets, although there are significant differences among workers within cohorts.[14]

The third characteristic of social security that is important in appraising its economic effects is that it is a diverse package of benefits—pension benefits for retired workers, disability benefits for workers suffering from long-term and total incapacity to work, dependents' benefits for certain relatives of retirees and the disabled, and survivors' benefits for dependent spouses and children of deceased workers.

The fourth characteristic that clearly differentiates social security from simple annuities and that is central to an understanding of the effects of the system on both labor supply and savings is the fact that beneficiaries are subject to an earnings test. Benefits paid to people younger than age seventy-two (age seventy beginning in 1983) are reduced by 50 percent of the excess of earnings over stipulated levels.[15]

---

88 (November 1974), pp. 551–73 reaches similar conclusions on theoretical grounds, but his analysis points out the possibility that changes in the amount of labor supplied can result in the shifting of some part of the burden of the payroll tax to other factors of production. The central conclusion of these analyses is that there is no analytical reason to suppose that the incidence of the portion of the payroll tax levied on employers is different from that of the portion levied on employees. Evidence is accumulating that the labor supply of older workers—both the number of hours worked and the decision when to retire—is more elastic than that of younger workers and that, as a result, the payroll tax may have some small effect on wage rates.

13. This issue is examined in chapter 6 under the section entitled "Effects on the Life-Cycle Distribution of Income."

14. Robert Moffitt, "Trends in Social Security Wealth by Cohort," paper prepared for the National Bureau of Economic Research Conference on Income and Wealth, Madison, Wisconsin, May 14–15, 1982.

15. The earnings test applies to retirement and survivors' benefits. Earnings up to $6,000 for people aged sixty-five to seventy-one and up to $4,440 for younger beneficiaries do not affect benefits. These limits rise with average earnings in the economy.

Future benefits may increase whenever earnings cause current benefits to be reduced. First, as noted above, benefits for retirees (and, in some instances, for their dependents) who are sixty-two to seventy-two are adjusted for any month in which benefits are reduced because of earnings. Second, work by beneficiaries may increase their benefits if earnings in the current year are higher than the earnings during at least one of the years used in computing average earnings. This highly technical feature of the system, which few people understand fully, has a large real effect on the value of benefits each worker can expect to receive. By requiring that the earnings of each worker be indexed before basic benefits are computed, the 1977 amendments reduced, but did not eliminate, the value of this adjustment.

Fifth, unlike any privately available annuity, social security benefits are fully indexed. Earnings histories and the benefit formula are indexed to wages, and currently payable benefits are indexed to prices. Thus social security provides a form of protection no other single asset now provides.

Some Special Terms

Among the technical terms that stud the literature on social security, three—"pay-as-you-go," "actuarially fair," and "mature"—deserve special comment. These terms are important because they are frequently used and because they are interrelated.[16]

A pay-as-you-go social security system is one in which annual revenues dedicated to the system approximately equal annual expenditures. Although it accumulated a modest reserve in its early years and that reserve is now declining, the U.S. social security system is essentially a pay-as-you-go system. An actuarially fair system promises to each cohort of workers entering the system benefits of the same present expected value as the taxes it will collect from them.[17] A mature pay-as-

16. In the special case in which the interest rate equals the growth of money wages, the applicability of any two guarantees the applicability of the third; as a corollary, if any one of these terms does not apply to a social security system, at least one of the others also does not apply.

17. Note that this definition permits the term "actuarially fair" to be applied to a system, like that in the United States, that provides to some workers within a cohort higher benefits relative to taxes paid or to earnings received than it provides to other workers. Thus the U.S. system can be regarded as actuarially fair, even if the progressive benefit formula is retained. A stricter definition would reserve the term "actuarially fair" for systems that provide each worker with benefits equal in value to taxes paid.

you-go system is one in which all retirees have paid taxes during their entire working life in covered employment to support the same system under which they will draw benefits.[18]

Thus an immature pay-as-you-go system (such as the U.S. system has been) must be actuarially unfair in the sense that many or all entering workers will receive benefits with greater present expected value than the taxes they will have to pay. This excess benefit is sometimes called a "lifetime wealth increment" in the literature on social security. It is possible for the lifetime wealth increment to be negative—that is, for the expected value of taxes to exceed the expected value of benefits—for example, if benefits are legislatively reduced or if the beneficiary belongs to a disfavored group.[19] But the lifetime wealth increment in the United States has been positive and large for all workers who have reached or will reach retirement in the twentieth century.[20] This excess of actual benefits over those that would be actuarially equivalent to the taxes workers have paid arose and continues to arise because Congress stipulated that benefits should begin in 1940, only three years after payroll taxes were first collected. Furthermore, Congress has periodically liberalized benefits and extended them to retirees, either immediately after they were enacted or well before workers could have fully earned them with increased taxes.

18. Maturity also depends on such other matters as population structure and life expectancies. Such a system provides an implicit rate of return on tax premiums approximately equal to the sum of the rates of growth of population and of real wages. See Paul A. Samuelson, "An Exact Consumption-Loan Model of Interest with or without the Social Contrivance of Money," *Journal of Political Economy*, vol. 66 (December 1958), pp. 467–82; and Henry J. Aaron, "The Social Insurance Paradox," *Canadian Journal of Economics and Political Science*, vol. 32 (August 1966), pp. 371–77.

19. As long as the social security system never terminates, it is possible that no cohort will ever experience a negative lifetime wealth increment even if early cohorts receive positive ones. The "debt" that these early transfers generate can be carried forward indefinitely.

20. Some authors have alleged that workers who have entered the labor force in the last ten years or so who will retire early in the twenty-first century and workers who enter the labor force in the future will receive benefits worth less than the taxes they will pay. A sufficient reduction in benefits could guarantee this outcome. See Michael J. Boskin and others, "Modelling Alternative Solutions to the Long-Run Social Security Funding Problem," a paper presented at the NBER Conference on Simulation Methods in Tax Policy Analysis, Palm Beach, Florida, January 26, 1981; Martin S. Feldstein and Anthony Pellechio, "Social Security Wealth: The Impact of Alternative Inflation Adjustments," *Policy Analysis with Social Security Research Files*, Research Report 52 (Social Security Administration, 1978), pp. 693–714. Although these estimates are carefully prepared, they do not support the contention that social security is actuarially unfair, because they attach

The Plan of the Book

The remainder of this book is divided into three parts. Chapter 2 examines the analytical models that economists have used to think about the economic effects of social security and to undergird their empirical estimates. It describes three rather abstract theoretical frameworks. Readers may find one or another of these models intuitively implausible or unappealing. However, an understanding of them will clarify the analysis of the economic effects of social security. Some readers may want to turn directly to chapters 3 through 6. Those chapters review trends on saving and on labor supply and evidence on the effects of social security on the distribution of income. The book concludes with some comments on the implications of this research on the immediate and long-term problems facing social security.

---

no value to important features of social security not available privately—such as complete indexing—and take no account of selling costs associated with virtually all private sector plans that provide roughly similar benefits. In contrast, simulations indicate that the internal rate of return on payroll taxes paid is positive for all cohorts under all demographic and economic assumptions used by the social security actuaries, if one assumes that all benefits promised under current law are paid and sufficient taxes are imposed to meet these obligations. See Louise Russell, *The Baby Boom Generation and the Economy* (Brookings Institution, 1982), chap. 6; and the section entitled "Effects on the Life-Cycle Distribution of Income" in chapter 6 below.

CHAPTER TWO

The Analytical Questions

THE theoretical debate about the economic effects of social security centers on one of the key unresolved analytical issues in economics, the question of how long a planning horizon individuals have and how much information they incorporate into their economic decisions. In addition to this central issue, the debate hinges on the degree to which a single theory can adequately represent the diverse behavior of many people in quite different stages of life and economic circumstances, with different levels of education, and from different cultural backgrounds.

There are three competing views about the degree to which people look into the future in making economic decisions. The most frequently used is the "life-cycle model," according to which people base their decisions about saving, labor supply, and other economically relevant actions on their anticipated lifetime wealth, earnings, and the rate of return on savings. Based on their preferences for leisure and consumption, now and at various points in the future, people decide how much to work, to consume, and, as a corollary of these two decisions, to save or dissave at each point in their adult lives.

In contrast to the life-cycle model, some economists hold that for many people and many decisions the planning horizon stretches only a few years or even months or days ahead.[1] Within this framework taxes, transfer payments, or other economic events set in the distant future have little or no impact on some or all current economic behavior. Still other economists hold that the actual planning horizons of most people are longer than the life cycle. According to this view, the fact that many people intentionally leave bequests, even small ones, signifies that they

1. A brief planning horizon may result for either of two reasons. First, for some people or for some decisions, the future may not count at all beyond a relatively brief period of time; in other words, the discount rate beyond some time in the future may be infinite. An almost equivalent result obtains if the planning horizon is formally infinite but the discount rate is high, because the high discount rate reduces to insignificance the importance of distant events.

benefit from the economic well-being of future generations and have multigeneration planning horizons.

This chapter is devoted to an explanation of why these three theories on how far ahead people look in making economic decisions figure prominently in the debate about the economic effects of social security. A number of other complicating circumstances should be kept in mind, however.

First, as the preceding description suggests, social security is complex. For analysts to estimate correctly its effects on economic behavior, they should incorporate in their theoretical and statistical models measures of taxes and benefits that match the perceptions or misperceptions of the people whose behavior is under study.[2] The most commonly used measure of this kind is social security wealth, the present expected value of future benefits.[3] The estimation of this quantity requires numerous strong assumptions that are explored in more detail below. In some theories of economic behavior this asset will influence individual and aggregate saving behavior, the timing of retirement, and possibly other aspects of labor supply.

A second complicating factor in appraising the economic effects of social security arises from the fact that people are diverse. It is commonplace for economists to posit a single norm that governs the behavior of

2. This statement is true only for certain problems. Suppose one measures the response to some variable, x, of which there are k units, and finds that people change their behavior along some dimension by m units. There is no way of deciding whether people correctly perceive x and respond at the rate m/k per unit of x or perceive, say, only half of the units of x ($k/2$ units) and respond at the rate $2m/k$. But in the case of a variable like social security wealth, which depends on perceptions of future benefits along many dimensions and on a discount rate, one cannot infer from the average measured response to social security wealth the response to specific changes in the underlying determinants of social security wealth. For example, a change in, say, the age at which unreduced benefits are paid that produced the same shift in social security wealth as, say, a change in the benefit formula might cause very different behavioral responses. If there were enough statistical degrees of freedom, one could incorporate a measure of each characteristic of the system; in that event, the various assumptions about perceptions used in measuring social security wealth would be unnecessary.

3. Present expected value is the discounted sum of a stream of payments, positive or negative, that occur at different times. The present value of a future payment is smaller than its nominal amount, because a smaller sum available now may be invested at prevailing rates of return and will accumulate to the larger future obligation. If the annual rate of interest is i, the present value of $1 payable n years in the future is $(1 + i)^{-n}$. Impatience, or time preference, also causes future obligations to be valued below present ones of equal nominal amount. If people can borrow or lend freely, they will do so until their rate of time preference, or willingness to trade present against future consumption, equals the rate of interest.

all people; the extended life-cycle model and the multigeneration model are examples.[4] But the general applicability of such models is assumed, not demonstrated. If empirical work rests on the assumptions of a pure model, but people in fact react as indicated by two or more different models, the resulting estimates may be biased.

The Life-Cycle Model

The life-cycle model of behavior suggests that individuals or families (the decisionmaking unit is not clear in the life-cycle model) decide on how much to work and how much to consume and to save based on actual and expected earnings, wealth, the rate of return on saving, and age. Economists developed the model because early Keynesian theory could not reconcile the behavior of individual consumers with time-series data on aggregate consumption.[5]

The theory has a number of important implications. It normally presumes that people plan to consume all of their income and wealth over their expected life cycles.[6] Observed bequests are thus unplanned, arising from the fact that people do not know when they will die. The theory predicts that consumers will save most of any windfall gain. It also predicts that retirees will dissave and that older people will immediately consume a larger fraction of a windfall than will younger people. In both cases, the theory holds that people will treat the windfall as if it were an increase in wealth.

The predictions of the model about the effects on saving of a rise in the real rate of return are ambiguous.[7]

4. Martin S. Feldstein, "Social Security, Induced Retirement, and Aggregate Capital Accumulation," *Journal of Political Economy,* vol. 82 (September–October 1974), pp. 905–26; and Robert J. Barro, "Are Government Bonds Net Wealth?" *Journal of Political Economy,* vol. 84 (November–December 1974), pp. 1095–1117.

5. Franco Modigliani and Richard Brumberg, "Utility Analysis and the Consumption Function: An Interpretation of Cross-section Data," in Kenneth K. Kurihara, ed., *Post-Keynesian Economics* (Rutgers University Press, 1954); Albert Ando and Franco Modigliani, "The 'Life Cycle' Hypothesis of Saving: Aggregate Implications and Tests," *American Economic Review,* vol. 53 (March 1963), pp. 55–84; and M. J. Farrell, "The New Theories of the Consumption Function," *Economic Journal,* vol. 69 (December 1959), pp. 678–96.

6. A bequest motive can be grafted onto the life-cycle model, but to keep the model simple, it usually is not.

7. Increases in nominal rates of return net of tax that are just offset by increases in expected inflation have no effect on saving plans if the change in interest rates has no

To understand the effects of social security on saving and labor supply, according to the life-cycle model, one must distinguish the annuity-like aspects of the system from its other special features. If social security were a simple individual annuity, the life-cycle model would yield straightforward predictions of its effect on both saving and labor supply.[8] However, the special features thoroughly muddy the picture.

In examining the effects of the annuity-like features of social security, one should distinguish two cases. In the first, the present expected value of annuity benefits equals the present expected value of taxes, calculated according to expected mortality rates and a rate of interest that is

---

effect on real wealth holdings. If a rise in nominal interest rates reduces real wealth holdings, it will tend to increase saving.

A rise in the rate of return reduces the present cost of future consumption; and because the price of future consumption has declined, people will want more of it. But they will increase saving only if future consumption increases proportionately more than its price has fallen.

For example, a rise in the rate of return from 3 percent to 5 percent a year would enable a person to make a $1,000 purchase ten years hence by setting aside $613.91 today, rather than $762.40. A deposit of $762.40 will accumulate to $1,000 at 3 percent compounded annually for ten years. A deposit of $613.91 will accumulate to $1,000 at 5 percent compounded annually for ten years. The price effect will cause saving to decline if people increase future consumption from $1,000 to any amount less than $1,241.88 (equals $1,000 × 762.40 ÷ 613.91); and saving will rise if they decide to consume more than that. Thus the elasticity of future consumption with respect to its price must be greater than unity in absolute value for saving to increase.

An unexpected increase in the rate of return on saving has an additional effect on people who are net asset-holders (or net debtors). An increase in the rate of return on wealth directly enriches holders of assets whose yield has increased, tending to boost their consumption. People with fixed yield assets suffer a decline in wealth when the general rate of return rises, because the market value of their assets tends to drop, and they will tend to reduce consumption. The effects on debtors are the reverse of those on net asset-holders. Thus the net effect on saving of a rise in the rate of return is unclear on theoretical grounds.

Empirical research for many years yielded conflicting results on whether saving was affected by the rate of interest and, if so, what the effect was. Problems of handling inflation were particularly troublesome in measuring the real rate of return. Recent studies have found that the real interest rate elasticity of savings is positive. See Thorvaldur Gylfason, "Interest Rates, Inflation, and the Aggregate Consumption Function," *Review of Economics and Statistics,* vol. 63 (May 1981), pp. 233–45; and Michael J. Boskin, "Taxation, Saving, and the Rate of Interest," *Journal of Political Economy,* vol. 86 (April 1978), pt. 2, pp. S3–S27. For a review of the literature and conflicting views, see E. Philip Howrey and Saul H. Hymans, "The Measurement and Determination of Loanable-Funds Saving," *Brookings Papers on Economic Activity, 3:1978,* pp. 655–85.

8. Whether the predictions would be accurate as well as straightforward depends, of course, on whether the life-cycle model accurately portrays people's behavior.

generally agreed upon. The second case entails the analysis of the effects of benefits that exceed the value of taxes paid. In the United States and in most other countries, social security benefits have not only returned taxes paid with interest, but also have provided a "bonus" or lifetime wealth increment, arising from the fact that most workers to date have paid taxes for only a part of their working lives at rates sufficient to sustain the benefit formula prevailing when they claim benefits. This bonus eventually may turn out to be negative in the United States for some workers, particularly single persons or high-wage workers who receive smaller benefits relative to taxes paid than do low-wage workers and those with dependents.[9]

Benefits Equal Taxes

According to the life-cycle theory, a social security system that paid an annuity equal in value to taxes paid would have no effect on consumption or labor supply, and hence on welfare, as long as the taxes imposed were no greater than the amount that the person would have saved voluntarily and the interest rate equalled the rate of growth of total wages. Such a system would reduce personal saving by the amount of social security taxes; but whether or not it reduced national saving would depend on whether the social security system accumulated reserves or operated on a pay-as-you-go basis.

Even if taxes exceeded desired saving, social security would have no effects on consumption, labor supply, or the worker's welfare if the worker could borrow at the same rate used in computing social security benefits enough to maintain current consumption.[10] For active workers, taxes would reduce disposable income, but the increment in entitlement to benefits would exactly offset this payment. Thus workers would perceive no change in their real wages and would not change the amount of labor they would be willing to supply. They would reduce personal saving by the amount of the tax payment.

9. This issue is examined in some detail below under the heading "Effects within Cohorts" in chapter 6. Viewing these gains and losses retrospectively ignores the insurance value to young workers who seldom know for sure whether they will have a lifetime of high or low earnings, whether they will be married, divorced, widowed, or never-married when they claim benefits, and whether they will have children or become disabled before age sixty-five.

10. See Alan S. Blinder, "Private Pensions and Public Pensions: Theory and Fact," a paper prepared as background for the W. S. Woytinsky Lecture, delivered in Washington, D.C., December 28, 1981.

The effect of social security on saving, according to the life-cycle model, depends on whether social security operates on a funded or pay-as-you-go basis. If the social security system amasses a reserve equal in present value to future benefit obligations and if other tax and government spending activities are independent of social security taxes and benefits, this flow of revenue will increase the government surplus (or reduce the government deficit), exactly offsetting with increased public saving (or with reduced public dissaving) the reduction in saving by covered workers. If social security operates on a pay-as-you-go basis, it will reduce total saving. The reduction is equal to the interest earnings on reserves that would have been generated in a fully funded system.

An actuarially fair annuity would leave consumption of beneficiaries unaffected, whether the system was funded or operated on a pay-as-you-go basis. Instead of depleting accumulated private assets, beneficiaries would draw social security benefits. Because the consumption of both workers and beneficiaries is unaffected, aggregate consumption is unchanged also by actuarially fair social security.

Benefits Greater Than Taxes

To the extent that people receive benefits greater than the taxes they have paid, evaluated at a market interest rate, the life-cycle model suggests that a simple annuity system will affect consumption, saving, and labor supply. The excess of future benefit entitlements over payments plus market interest looks to the worker like a wage increase that takes the form of a noncashable asset. The effect of such a wage increase on labor supply depends on the form in which the lifetime wealth increment is provided. A liberalization of the benefit formula, so that each additional dollar of earnings generates a larger pension, may raise or lower labor supply. Such a liberalization is equivalent to a rise in the wage rate.[11] The higher remuneration at the margin makes additional work more attractive, but the increase in total income encourages people to seek more leisure.[12] Whether labor supply rises or falls depends on

11. The text refers to a change in the formula relating benefits, B, to earnings, E, from $B = f(E)$ to $B = af(E)$, where $a > 1$.

12. These offsetting effects are the economist's familiar substitution and income effects. Their combined effect is the total wage elasticity of labor supply, which may be positive or negative. It is worth noting that additional leisure is not necessarily a good for all people, and additional work is not necessarily a burden. Thus the income effect need not be negative.

which of these two effects predominates. A liberalization that provides a larger benefit at each earnings level, but does not increase the rate at which benefits rise as earnings increase, tends to encourage earlier retirement.[13] Benefits may be liberalized by different amounts at different ages, further complicating the story, but leaving unaltered the ambiguous effect on labor supply. The effects of reductions in benefits are the mirror image of those of benefit increases.

Increases in benefit entitlements that exceed tax payments increase consumption unambiguously and reduce saving, according to the life-cycle model. The worker perceives that he has received a wage increase, all in the form of a future annuity. Normally he would choose to consume part of any increase in income. To achieve this purpose, he would reduce voluntary saving or increase borrowing to increase current consumption.

The U.S. social security system is an immature, pay-as-you-go system that has provided lifetime wealth increments to all workers who have retired thus far. As such, according to the life-cycle model, it would tend to have reduced saving, apart from certain features described below.

Capital Market Imperfections

The foregoing examples take for granted either that workers pay tax premiums for their annuities no greater than they would have saved voluntarily, or that they are able to borrow enough at the same interest rate used in computing the value of social security benefits to achieve their desired distributions of consumption over time.

These conditions may not be satisfied, however. Even if the expected value of benefits always equals taxes, the system may affect saving or labor supply. For example, some people, particularly those whose incomes are low or lower than they expect them to be in the future, may voluntarily save nothing and exhaust all borrowing opportunities to

13. In this case the formula changes from $B = f(E)$ to $B = f(E) + k$, where $k > 0$ and therefore there is an income effect, but no substitution effect. For an analysis of these cases, See Gary Burtless and Robert A. Moffitt, "Social Security and the Retirement Decision: A Graphical Analysis," and "The Effects of Social Security on the Labor Supply of the Aged: The Joint Choice of Retirement Date and Post Retirement Hours of Work." Both papers are part of the Brookings Institution Project on Research in Retirement and Aging, funded by the Office of Planning and Evaluation, Department of Health and Human Services. Also see Olivia S. Mitchell and Gary S. Fields, "The Effects of Pensions and Earnings on Retirement: A Review Essay," National Bureau of Economic Research Working Paper 772, September 1981.

finance current consumption. In that event, social security taxes reduce current consumption of workers and have no effect on their saving. Beneficiaries who have no assets and who consume all income are in a similar position. To the extent that taxes are levied on the former to pay benefits to the latter, these effects will offset each other, and saving will be unaffected. If taxes exceed benefits in the aggregate, leading to increases in accumulated surplus (or reserves), total saving will increase; if benefits exceed taxes, saving will be reduced. The effect occurs to the extent that people do not voluntarily alter saving when income changes.

Workers in such a situation would probably view the introduction or increase of social security as a wage reduction, even if future benefits, evaluated at some market rate of interest, were worth as much as taxes. The frustrated desire to consume more income now signifies relatively low valuation of the future consumption that a social security annuity would enable.

The Nonannuity Aspects of Social Security

As the background description of social security made clear, social security differs from a simple annuity,[14] and these aspects cloud the simple predictions of the life-cycle model about its effects on saving and labor supply. Social security provides many benefits besides simple retirement benefits. In 1981, 8.1 percent of benefit payments under the old age, survivors, and disability insurance program went to disabled workers and their dependents, 71.5 percent to retired workers, and 20.4 percent to relatives of retirees.[15] These benefits serve some of the functions performed in part by workmen's compensation, term life insurance, ordinary life insurance, and private disability plans, as well as by other forms of private saving.

14. In one respect, social security in the United States is more like an annuity than any privately available pension, insurance policy, or combination of investments. Because social security benefits are now automatically and fully adjusted for inflation, they constitute an assured, constant real income. No fully indexed private asset is available in the United States, so that the real return on private annuities is always risky. Packages of private investments historically have come close to tracking price increases, but they have yielded no significant positive rate of return. See Zvi Bodie, "Investment Strategy in an Inflationary Environment," in Benjamin Friedman, ed., *The Changing Roles of Debt and Equity in Financing U.S. Capital Formation* (University of Chicago Press, 1982), pp. 47–64.

15. Social Security Administration, *Social Security Bulletin,* vol. 45 (Government Printing Office, April 1982), tables M-5, M-6, and M-11, pp. 15, 16, 21.

Of greater importance, social security benefits are related not just to past earnings, but also to current earnings through the earnings test, the actuarial adjustment of benefits of people affected by the earnings test, and the recomputation of benefits to incorporate the effect of current earnings on wage histories. These provisions may directly encourage or discourage early retirement and voluntary saving, according to the analytical implications of the life-cycle model.

If one concentrates on the reduction in current benefits for those who work past age sixty-two and who earn enough to cause some reduction in their benefits (more than $4,440 for beneficiaries aged sixty-two to sixty-four, $6,000 for beneficiaries who are sixty-five or older), the reduction of benefits may either raise or lower labor supply and savings. The direct effect of the benefit cut is to lower the expected value of lifetime benefits. This feature of the system has the effect of lowering the net wage for additional work by people subject to the retirement income test. If the test lowers labor supply, it will increase saving if it lengthens the period spent in retirement, because, as first pointed out by Martin Feldstein, an increased period spent in retirement will raise the proportion of lifetime resources that should not be consumed as earned (in other words, that should be saved) and, unless social security benefits meet all needs for income during retirement, saving would tend to rise.[16]

The existence of actuarial adjustments in the benefit formula and of benefit recomputation complicate the story greatly, however. For workers aged sixty-two to sixty-four, benefits are increased by 8⅓ percent of the amount payable at age sixty-two *on a given earnings history* for each year that a worker earns enough to be denied any benefits.[17] This adjustment is sufficient so that the expected value of benefits over a lifetime is negligibly affected for an average worker. In addition, however, earnings of workers eligible for retirement benefits who are subject to the earnings test are used to recompute the workers' earnings histories if such recomputation increases benefits.[18] This recomputation, coming on top of the actuarial adjustment, means that work by people aged sixty-two to sixty-four is likely to increase the expected value of lifetime

16. Feldstein, "Social Security, Induced Retirement, and Aggregate Capital Accumulation," pp. 919–20.

17. Actually future benefits are increased by 25/36 of 1 percent (1/12 of 8⅓ percent) for each month in which benefits are reduced by even one dollar. See chapter 1, note 8.

18. Because of administrative problems, automatic recomputation and the attendant increase in benefits are subject to lengthy delays. However, workers may secure recomputation promptly if they file an explicit request.

social security benefits.[19] No one knows how well workers understand the actuarial adjustments and benefit recomputation and hence whether they respond to real or imagined economic incentives.

For workers aged sixty-five to seventy-two, the logic is unchanged, but benefits are increased by only 3 percent of the benefits payable at age sixty-five for each year during which benefits are completely withheld. The degree to which this adjustment, together with benefit recomputation, offsets the reduction of payments for people whose earnings cause their benefits to be reduced varies from worker to worker.[20] It is clear, however, that such adjustments at least partly offset the reductions.

The foregoing analysis reveals that it is not clear whether social security, viewed through the life-cycle model, in theory should have any effect on labor supply or saving and, if it does, whether the effects should be positive or negative.[21] Furthermore, despite its obvious intellectual appeal, many economists hold that the life-cycle model poorly portrays how people make plans. Some stress that the planning horizon is longer, some shorter, than is assumed in the life-cycle model and build their analysis on those assumptions.

Evidence on the validity of the life-cycle model is mixed. A major puzzle is the failure of people to dissave as much after retirement as the life-cycle model would suggest.[22] A bequest motive could explain the

19. See Alan S. Blinder, Roger H. Gordon, and Donald E. Wise, *An Empirical Study of the Effect of Pensions and the Saving and Labor Supply Decisions of Older Men,* (Princeton: MATHTECH, March 30, 1981) and "Reconsidering the Work Disincentive Effects of Social Security," *National Tax Journal,* vol. 33 (December 1980). Richard V. Burkhauser and John A. Turner challenge the validity of the calculations by Blinder, Gordon, and Wise in "Can Twenty-Five Million Americans Be Wrong?—A Response to Blinder, Gordon, and Wise," *National Tax Journal,* vol. 34 (December 1981), pp. 467–72. See also Alan S. Blinder, Roger H. Gordon, and Donald H. Wise, "Rhetoric and Reality in Social Security Analysis—A Rejoinder," *National Tax Journal,* vol. 34 (December 1981), pp. 473–78.

20. See note 19.

21. For an application of this model, together with an unusually clear demonstration of why the results are ambiguous, see Burtless and Moffitt, "Social Security and the Retirement Decision" and "The Effects of Social Security on the Labor Supply of the Aged."

22. Sheldon Danziger and others state: "The elderly not only do not dissave to finance their consumption during retirement, they spend less on consumption goods and services (and save significantly more) than the nonelderly at all levels of income. Moreover, the oldest of the elderly save the most at given levels of income." See their "The Life-Cycle Hypothesis and the Consumption Behavior of the Elderly," Brookings Institution Project on Research in Retirement and Aging, sponsored by the Office of Planning and Evaluation,

presence of terminal wealth, but not the failure to dissave. Old people might fail to dissave if they fear future contingencies, such as invalidism and the need to pay for nursing home care, against which they cannot or do not want to insure and for which they accumulate or maintain assets.[23] But this explanation undermines the predictive value of the life-cycle model by hinging behavior on motivations that are quite separate from the basic theory.[24] The life-cycle model also seems unable to explain most of the observed variation among people in consumption and saving behavior and, as will be indicated below, it does not lead to clear empirical estimates of the effects of pensions or of social security.[25]

The Multigeneration Model

The big puzzle for the life-cycle model is why people leave bequests or make gifts. A second big puzzle is why the model explains so little of the variation of savings reported in household surveys. Some elderly people leave bequests to children and to others. Others receive aid from children. Those who live with children may give or receive financial aid, on balance. The multigeneration model rests on the proposition that social security will affect these flows by increasing bequests by the elderly and diminishing the gifts they receive.

---

the Department of Health and Human Services. See also Mordecai Kurz, "The Effects of Social Security and Private Pensions on Family Savings" (Menlo Park, California: SRI International, April 22, 1981); Thad Mirer, "The Dissaving Behavior of the Retired Aged," *Southern Economic Journal*, vol. 46 (April 1980), pp. 1197–1205 and "The Wealth-Age Relationship among the Aged," *American Economic Review*, vol. 69 (June 1979), pp. 435–43; both studies report that there is relatively little dissaving, or even net accumulation, among the aged. In contrast, Peter Diamond and Jerry Hausman, "Individual Savings Behavior," a paper prepared for the National Commission on Social Security, May 1980, use other data to estimate some evidence of dissaving among the aged.

23. Such behavior would result also if the elderly anticipate that their tastes will change, so that consumption will be more satisfying in the future; but such an explanation seems implausible.

24. It is possible that people who make very long-term plans might not dissave for a number of reasons. Social security might induce such people to hold less wealth at each age than they would if social security did not exist. This example illustrates that validity of the life-cycle model is neither a necessary nor a sufficient condition for social security to affect saving.

25. See chapters 4 and 5.

Bequests Given

To some degree, as noted above, bequests would result even if everyone behaved as the life-cycle model suggests and intended to leave nothing to heirs, because people seldom know exactly when they will die and because private annuities yield uncertain and low real rates of return.[26] But many people leave bequests intentionally; some evidence suggests that the desire to accumulate assets for bequests may account for a large share of private saving in the United States.[27]

It is easy to posit a variety of motives for bequests. For example, some people may seek to extend their own power and influence beyond their natural lives through gifts to charities, family members, or others. Some people may wish to bind progeny or other relatives to themselves during life with the promise of a postmortem gift. Others may wish simply to leave pleasant memories of themselves through a final act of generosity. Some may value additional current consumption less than the pleasure of accumulating wealth. In short, the testator may draw satisfaction from leaving the bequest, not from the anticipated pleasure from consumption by the heirs.

None of these motives, however, plays any part in the most widely cited multigeneration model used to analyze the effects of social security on economic behavior. Rather, each person is presumed to derive satisfaction from the consumption by people to whom bequests are made and to equalize the marginal personal satisfaction of the last dollar spent on personal consumption with that of the last dollar devoted to bequests.[28] Thus if a man would enjoy greater satisfaction from bequeathing one dollar more to someone than from consuming it himself (now or in the future), he would save one dollar more to increase his bequests. He may save also for life-cycle reasons—for example, to provide income during retirement—but the bequest motive is also present.[29]

26. The fact that rates of return under annuities are low means that people will accept increased risk as the price for higher rates of return on other investments.

27. Laurence J. Kotlikoff and Lawrence H. Summers, "The Role of Intergenerational Transfers in Aggregate Capital Accumulation," *Journal of Political Economy,* vol. 89 (August 1981), pp. 706–32.

28. These motives can be accommodated in the earlier theory of Alan Blinder, "Intergenerational Transfers and Life Cycle Consumption," *American Economic Review,* vol. 66 (May 1976, *Papers and Proceedings, December 1975*), pp. 87–93.

29. Through this process the model postulates that this generation takes into account

Hinging the bequest motive solely on the indirect satisfaction that people draw from the consumption by their heirs is central to the analysis of the economic effects of social security. Like the life-cycle model, the multigeneration model predicts no economic effects from a social security system that returns to each worker expected benefits worth just as much as the taxes paid. Unlike the life-cycle model, however, the multigeneration model also predicts that there will be no aggregate effect on the economic behavior of people who receive benefits worth more or less than the taxes they have paid in, because they adjust bequests to offset the lifetime wealth increments that they receive.[30]

Gifts Received

The fact that few people today leave significant bequests or did so in the past seems to undermine the model; but its advocates point out that social security has the effect of reducing the aid that children in past

---

the economic standing of all future generations in perpetuity in making saving and consumption decisions today. This result follows as a result of a chain: generation A cares about both its own consumption and the welfare of generation B, which cares about both its own consumption and the welfare of generation C, and so on, ad infinitum.

30. To simplify the central argument, suppose that all people are identical and that social security treats identically all people of the same age, paying them benefits worth more than the taxes they have paid. Each member of this cohort receives a windfall that, according to the life-cycle model, would affect economic behavior. According to the multigeneration model, it does not because the advent of a system paying benefits worth more than tax payments results in the creation of a debt for future generations to service and perhaps to pay. Each member of the current generation is aware that this social security windfall has increased the amount that he or she can consume and decreased the amount available to future generations. If each such person had previously established the optimum bequest, balancing the direct utility of personal consumption with the indirect satisfaction from the incremental consumption by heirs made possible by the bequest, the advent of the social security windfall will upset the balance. By adding to the wealth of the present generation, social security enables those who receive the windfall to increase consumption, permitting them to move to items with lower marginal value; it simultaneously limits the consumption of later generations, restricting them to higher priority items.

If that were the end of the story, social security windfalls would affect economic behavior in the fashion suggested by the life-cycle model. According to the multigeneration model, however, people change their bequests to offset the windfall. They increase bequests by exactly the amount of the windfall, reestablishing thereby the balance between the marginal satisfaction from their own consumption and the indirect satisfaction that they derive from the consumption by their heirs. Thus people increase personal saving to offset the decline in public saving (or the increase in public debt) that arises from the payment of social security benefits worth more than the taxes they paid.

generations provided their aged parents. Social security thus relieves children of a "negative bequest" from their parents. In addition, it is alleged, social security can alter transfers between generations not merely by changing bequests, but also by influencing the "investments" people make in the education of their children and their gifts to friends and relatives.

There is considerable evidence that reliance by the elderly on their children has declined since the advent of social security benefits. To the extent that social security reduces transfers from others to the elderly, it leaves the consumption possibilities of the elderly unchanged, and the relief for the nonelderly from transfers they would otherwise feel obligated to make represents an immediate offset to the payroll taxes they pay, leaving their consumption unaffected.

It is still possible for social security to affect behavior within the multigeneration model because not all people are alike, because social security is not a uniform annuity, and because the national debt is held collectively rather than apportioned with precision among the population. Thus, an immature pay-as-you-go social security system that provides the early cohorts of retirees with benefits worth more than the taxes they paid creates a debt for future generations; but the size of the windfall that workers receive may differ from the share of the debt that they perceive their heirs to bear.

It is worth noting that social security would not be so lacking in effects on saving and labor supply if bequests were presumed to be motivated by reasons other than the desire of people to equalize the marginal utility of their own direct consumption with their indirect satisfaction from the consumption by their heirs. For example, the desire to bind heirs or to do a final act of kindness can be satisfied with a bequest of a given size; to the extent that these motives for bequests are governing, a windfall arising from social security benefits worth more than the taxes paid might affect consumption and saving and, perhaps, labor supply as well.

The Short-Horizon Model

The life-cycle and multigeneration models both assume that people behave with complete rationality based on the best available information and that they formulate plans covering long periods of time. The strength of this assumption of rationality is that it enables analysts to bring the full armory of economic theory to bear on the question of how social security affects economic behavior. The weakness is the belief of many economists and the conviction of most others that people do not consistently make rational lifetime plans as posited by these models.

People might not behave with the requisite degree of rationality for two rather different reasons. First, people might behave irrationally, in the sense that their behavior follows no consistent set of rules or preferences. None of the social sciences is built on the assumption that people are consistently irrational, and it is hard to imagine how systematic analysis could proceed on such an assumption.

Second, people might behave rationally, but use a much shorter planning horizon for most decisions than is assumed by the life-cycle or muligeneration models. They might look only a relatively brief period ahead—measured in weeks, months, or a small number of years— because their information on the future is so poor that they believe efforts to plan into the distant future will yield little and because they fear that serious efforts to plan into the distant future are impossibly complex. They might use different planning horizons for different kinds of decisions or at different ages, depending on the cost of making long-term plans, the quality of available information, and the consequences of errors.

Alternatively, they might use a long planning horizon, but discount the future so heavily that events more than a few years into the future, although taken into account, have little subjective importance. People who heavily discount the future would be expected not to save, but to borrow to the maximum possible extent, probably up to credit limits.[31] They would be expected to approach retirement with few or no voluntarily accumulated assets. If tastes change systematically as people grow older, so that people plan farther into the future as they grow older, or so that a fixed planning horizon comes to encompass years after retirement, one would expect people to find themselves with "too few" assets in their later years and to increase saving sharply as they grow older.[32]

Short-horizon models are theoretically inelegant because they leave unexplained why people choose whatever planning horizon they use.

31. The implications would be that their subjective rates of time preference much exceed any interest rate they face on borrowing or could obtain on investments.

32. A similar pattern results if the life-cycle model holds, if capital markets are imperfect so that people cannot borrow against future income, and if income rises with age.

Some economists have tried to explain why full use of all information may not make economic sense. Processing all information may yield gains too small to justify the effort, causing people to adopt rules of thumb that allow them to achieve acceptable outcomes.[33] In other cases the cost of obtaining information causes people intentionally and rationally to make imperfect decisions. But until such time as economic theorists incorporate into the main line of economic analysis an explanation of why people behaving rationally choose short planning horizons (perhaps because of uncertainty about the future or information costs), this model will play a small role in economic analysis, however much it seems to accord with observed shortsightedness.

The analysis of the economic effects of social security that emerges from the short-horizon model differs greatly from that rooted in the life-cycle or multigeneration models in several respects. In its extreme form the short-horizon model posits that people look only one period (usually a year) ahead. In this extreme form the model suggests that social security appears to be a "tax-transfer" system, imposing taxes on workers, most of whom place no value on the future benefits they are acquiring because they will receive benefits beyond their relevant planning horizon or discount them so heavily that they have little subjective value. Thus for workers who earn less than the taxable maximum, social security is equivalent to a reduction in the wage rate. The effect on labor supply of a wage rate reduction is theoretically indeterminate, as noted above, although the most recent evidence suggests that net wage rate reductions for prime-age workers reduce labor supply slightly.[34] For workers who earn more than the maximum earnings level subject to tax, the social security tax unambiguously increases labor supply because it lowers disposable income without reducing the marginal return to work.

By reducing disposable income, the tax unambiguously tends to reduce consumption by all workers, according to the short-horizon model. For workers who ignore the accumulation of social security

33. The first economist to suggest that this form of behavior is widespread was Herbert Simon; other models have been developed by Richard Cyert and James March, among others. For an interesting effort to incorporate irrational beliefs into a standard analytical framework based on utility maximization, see George A. Akerlof and William T. Dickens, "The Economic Consequences of Cognitive Dissonance," *Amercian Economic Review*, vol. 72 (June 1982), pp. 307–19.

34. Jerry A. Hausman, "Labor Supply," in Henry J. Aaron and Joseph A. Pechman, eds., *How Taxes Affect Economic Behavior* (Brookings Institution, 1981), pp. 27–72.

entitlements, the future availability of benefits does not affect current consumption or saving independently of the effect of the tax on income.

For beneficiaries the effects are opposite. When younger, workers did not take account of future benefits in planning saving or labor supply; so benefits raise nonwage income and unambiguously reduce labor supply in the short-horizon model. This effect might be offset to the extent that current work raises future benefits and workers recognize such future increases in their current plans. The rise in income increases consumption of beneficiaries.

Taking the effects on both workers and beneficiaries into account, the short-horizon model suggests that pay-as-you-go social security would have little or no effect on consumption. Such effects would arise only to the extent that taxpayers and beneficiaries consume different proportions of income at the margin or to the extent that benefit payments and taxes differ. According to this model, social security would probably reduce the labor supply of workers (by lowering the net wage) and of beneficiaries (by boosting income).

In less extreme forms, the short-horizon model suggests merely that most people make plans for much less than a full lifetime, but allows for the possibility that planning horizons may vary with age. Thus social security would be little more than a tax for young workers. At a certain age, however, workers might begin to plan for retirement and to recognize the value of entitlements to social security benefits. Such a model would suggest conclusions like those of the life-cycle model, but only for older workers.[35]

Summary

Despite the complexity of the incentives created by social security sketched above, the actual effects are vastly more complex than indicated so far. The reason is that social security affects the economy indirectly in many ways.

For example, if social security reduces saving and the capital stock, there will be less capital per worker, the equilibrium rate of return to investment will tend to rise, and the equilibrium wage rate will fall. If there were no resulting flow of capital among nations in response to

35. A framework like this one is implicit in Alicia H. Munnell, *The Effect of Social Security on Personal Saving* (Ballinger, 1974).

variations in the rate of return, the effects of all changes in saving would be reflected in the domestic economy. One study suggests that differences in saving rates among nations translate dollar-for-dollar into differences in investment, but recent work has shown that the tests employed in that study were invalid.[36] On the other hand, if capital flowed freely among countries in pursuit of the highest rate of return, measures to increase saving in one country would have small effects on domestic capital formation unless such policies were matched with measures to increase domestic investment. Although capital today moves internationally with greater ease than it did in the years immediately following World War II, obstacles still remain; for that reason, the truth lies somewhere between the two extremes. To the still unknown extent that capital moves internationally in pursuit of the highest rate of return, any effects of social security on saving would not translate into equivalent changes in domestic capital formation.

Second, the fact that the age of entitlement to retirement benefits in social security was originally age sixty-five explains in part why many private pensions provide for a similar "retirement age." Private pensions do not actuarially adjust benefits routinely for continued work past the age of entitlement, nor are most benefits recomputed as they are under social security.[37] Continued work thus frequently reduces the value of private pension benefits. To the extent that the choice of sixty-five as the age of private pension entitlement is attributable to social security, behavior is indirectly altered by a legislative feature of social security. But the direct stimulus is the private pension system.

36. Feldstein and Horioka argue that rises in domestic saving do not leak abroad, but rather result in almost dollar-for-dollar increases in domestic investment. See Martin Feldstein and Charles Horioka, "Domestic Saving and International Capital Flows," *Economic Journal,* vol. 90 (June 1980), pp. 314–29. However, their analysis did not constitute a meaningful test. Barry Bosworth reports that, because of the methods used in most foreign countries to compile statistics on saving and investment, Feldstein and Horioka estimated a statistical identity, a meaningless procedure. See Bosworth, "Capital Formation and Economic Policy," *Brookings Papers on Economic Activity, 2:1982,* forthcoming.

37. The story is actually a good deal more complicated. "Defined contribution" plans, in which workers have what amounts to special savings accounts from which pensions will be paid and which served about 15 percent of all workers with pensions in 1975, are actuarially adjusted in the sense that the size of the benefit is related to the age at which payment begins, based on tables of life expectancies and interest earned after entitlement. "Defined benefit" plans, which serve at least 85 percent of all workers with pensions, normally pay a fixed amount based in some way on average wages (frequently during the final few years of service) and length of service. The proportion of workers dependent

The rather meandering journey just completed through three theoretical models widely used for thinking about the effects of social security on economic behavior makes two points clear—that a person determined to find a respected theoretical argument to support a preconception can find one, and that a person without preconceptions will find a bewildering diversity of answers in economic theory about whether social security is more likely to raise or to lower consumption or labor supply.

To get by this theoretical impasse, one turns with hope to empirical research for measures of observed behavioral responses. As will become clear, most of these hopes remain unfulfilled. Empirical research to date suggests that no one model explains the behavior of all households, and it has not succeeded in producing reliable estimates of the effects on behavior of any of the major policies.

---

primarily on defined contribution plans may be considerably smaller than 15 percent (though the proportion of defined contribution plans is increasing), as many persons have a defined-benefit plan as their primary plan, which they supplement with a defined-contribution or profit-sharing plan. These plans are not actuarially adjusted as benefits, once begun, are seldom indexed and never indexed completely and automatically. However, the amount of benefits paid each month to a worker who defers claiming them will increase if the delay lengthens the number of years of service used in computing the benefit or if wages are rising. The value of the increase in the amount of the monthly benefit may partly or completely offset the loss from deferral. On private pensions in general, see Alicia H. Munnell, *The Economics of Private Pensions* (Brookings Institution, 1982).

CHAPTER THREE

Historical Trends

NATIONAL saving and labor supply are subject to many influences other than social security. For this reason, it is necessary as part of a successful effort to measure the effects of social security on economic behavior simultaneously to control statistically for these other influences. It is also necessary to have an accurate measure of the size of the social security system to measure its influence.

Saving and Labor Supply

The problem can be approached in three ways. First, one can examine the various factors that determine aggregate saving or labor supply in a single country over time—time-series analysis. Second, one can examine the factors that determine how much households save or work at a given time—cross-sectional analysis. Third, one can try to identify the determinants of aggregate saving or labor supply in various countries at a given time—international cross-sectional analysis. A summary of the results of such studies performed in or on the United States appears in succeeding chapters.

Before turning to these studies, one should have a broad picture of the historical trends in saving and labor supply. These trends are displayed in figures 2 through 5.

Saving

Gross saving in the United States has shown no trend since World War II and is somewhat higher than it was during the 1930s (see figure 2).[1] Of the components of total saving, personal saving shows no

1. A regression of gross saving on a time trend yields an insignificant ($t = 0.85$), small negative coefficient (-0.019) from the first quarter of 1947 through the first quarter of 1981.

Figure 2. *Business Saving, Personal Saving, Government Saving, and Total Saving as a Percent of Gross National Product, 1929–80*

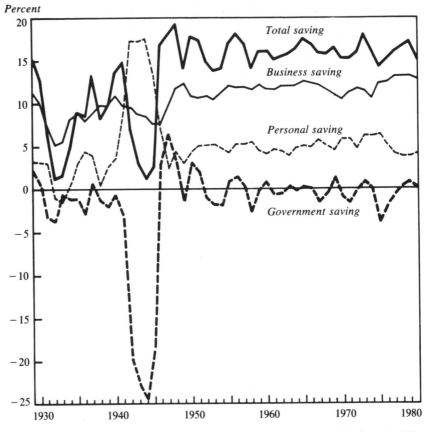

Sources: Bureau of Economic Analysis, *National Income and Product Accounts 1929–76* (GPO, September 1981), p. 195, and *Economic Report of the President, February 1982*, p. 262.

significant trend from 1947 to the latest year for which data are available.[2] Business saving has tended to increase slightly, and government saving has decreased.[3] If one subtracts depreciation from gross saving to obtain

2. The coefficient from a regression of personal saving on a time trend is 0.016 ($t = 1.08$).

3. The coefficients from regressions of business saving and government saving on a time trend are, respectively 0.042 ($t = 3.52$) and -0.0788 ($t = 2.77$). The simple correlation between government saving and total saving is high ($r^2 = 0.66$). Those between total saving and personal saving and total saving and business saving (0.02 and 0.00, respectively) are low.

Figure 3. *Net Saving, Net Private Saving, and Government Saving as a Percent of Net National Product, 1929–80*

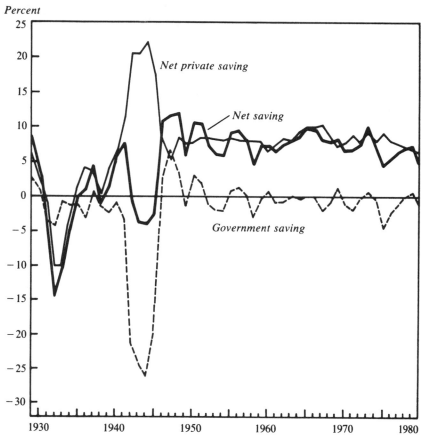

Source: Data provided by Edward F. Denison, Brookings Institution, and *Economic Report of the President, February 1982*, p. 262.

net saving, there is still no indication of a declining rate of saving (see figure 3).[4]

Labor Supply

The trends in labor force participation of men have been markedly different from those of women in the twentieth century (see figures 4 and

4. The average net private saving rate is 7.96 percent from 1948 to 1964 and 8.22 percent from 1965 to 1980. See Edward F. Denison, "Another Note on Private Saving," Washington, D.C., April 24, 1981.

Figure 4. *Labor Force Participation Rates for Men, 1900–79*[a]

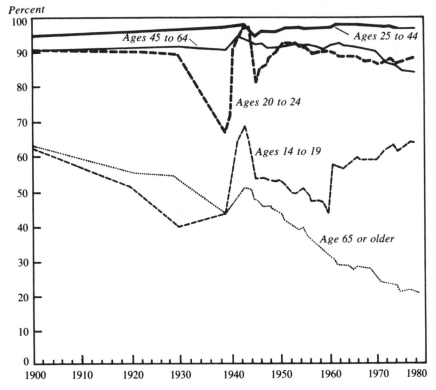

Sources: Bureau of the Census, *Historical Statistics of the United States, Colonial Times to 1970* (GPO, 1975), p. 132, and Bureau of Labor Statistics, *Handbook of Labor Statistics* (GPO, 1980), pp. 7–9.

a. The labor force participation rates for 1900 to 1940 are for the decennial years.

5). Except for the aberrational years from 1930 through 1946, which include the Great Depression and World War II, the participation rates of men aged forty-four or younger have remained stable or risen; the participation rate of men aged forty-five to sixty-four remained high and stable until the late 1960s when it began to fall, largely because of the withdrawal from the labor force of men aged fifty-five to sixty-four; and the participation rate of men aged sixty-five or older has declined throughout the twentieth century, although somewhat more rapidly after World War II than before (see figure 4).[5]

For females the story is one of increasing labor force participation,

5. The detail on the withdrawal from the labor force of men aged fifty-five to sixty-four is not shown in the figure.

Figure 5. *Labor Force Participation Rates for Women, 1900–79*[a]

Percent

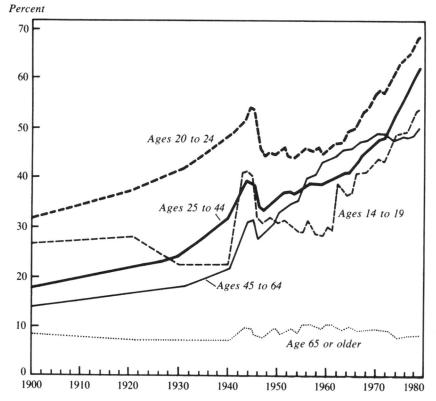

Sources: Same as figure 4.
a. Same as figure 4.

except by women aged sixty-five or older, whose participation in the labor force has been constant (see figure 5). The trend was interrupted only during the 1950s when women bore the children of the post–World War II baby boom and stayed home with them during their early childhood years. Little increase in the labor force participation of women aged sixty-five or older has occurred.

It is important to keep in mind that participation rates measure only one of many dimensions of labor supply. Others include hours and days worked per week, number of holidays per year, and work effort on the job.[6] Data on average hours per week are not compiled systematically

6. See Harvey S. Rosen, "What Is Labor Supply and Do Taxes Affect It?" *American Economic Review*, vol. 70 (May 1980, *Papers and Proceedings, December 1979*), pp. 171–76.

by age bracket, but the average for the nation has declined. Data on the number of holidays are scarce, but the trend almost certainly has been upward. Information on work effort, other than anecdotal, is lacking.

Interpretation of Trends

A casual observer of figures 2 through 5 might note the following. Saving has shown no trend in the United States over the period during which social security and other forms of contractual retirement income, such as pensions, have grown rapidly. It appears, therefore, that unless other factors tended to push up saving, social security has not had any perceptible effect on saving. Labor force participation, except among men aged sixty-five or older, has remained high and, in the case of women, has increased markedly.[7] Thus the amount of labor supplied by the typical family seems to be increasing, except in the case of elderly families where it seems to be declining (men decreasing, women constant).

The amount of labor supplied by elderly men has declined throughout the twentieth century, but the downward trend seems to have accelerated since World War II, when social security and private pensions became important. Part of the drop in labor force participation is probably attributable to rising income and the increased ability to afford retirement, and part to institutional change, such as the rise of social security and the spread of private pensions that has also occurred since World War II. Sorting out the relative importance of these factors requires more information than is contained in figures 4 and 5.

Measures of Social Security Wealth

A complex benefit schedule, actuarial adjustments, earnings tests, benefit recomputations, and the dependence of benefits on the possibility of future marriages, divorces, births, and deaths make it extraordinarily hard to calculate accurately the expected present value of future social security benefits for individuals or the nation. This problem lies at the core of all attempts to estimate the economic effects of social security

7. The participation of men aged fifty-five to sixty-four has also declined, from 86.9 percent in 1950 to 83 percent in 1970 and to 70.6 percent in 1981. This trend is not shown in figure 4 because statistics before 1947 are unavailable.

because one must be able to measure the relative size of social security benefits in order to estimate their effects. Some analysts have relied on current benefits to measure the social security stimulus; and it is arguable that this indicator, adjusted for predictable changes in coverage, is a good proxy for what workers think their benefits will be when they retire. However, expectations about changes in benefit amounts may also affect behavior.

To take account both of changes in coverage and of real benefits, economists commonly use a measure of the present expected value of social security benefits, or gross social security wealth, as a measure of influence of this governmental program on economic behavior;[8] for other purposes the present expected value of future payroll taxes is subtracted from gross social security wealth to yield net social security wealth. Social security wealth can be used either in time-series analyses of national aggregate saving or labor supply or in cross-sectional analyses of the saving and labor supply of individual families.

The methods of calculating social security wealth for time-series and cross-sectional analyses differ, but in all cases the analyst is forced to make a number of very strong and somewhat arbitrary assumptions. Because differences in estimates of social security wealth play some role in debates about the effects of social security on economic behavior, it is necessary to understand the nature of those assumptions.

If benefits continue to be fully indexed and if one can agree on an appropriate discount rate, it is easy to estimate social security wealth for current beneficiaries because actual benefits are known and the future changes in these benefits from actuarial adjustments and benefit recomputation can be estimated with little error.

Unfortunately, that is just the beginning of the story. Consider the social security wealth of a man aged thirty-five who is married and has one child. He may later become eligible for benefits if he becomes disabled or retires; and his family may become eligible for dependents' benefits while he lives and survivors' benefits after he dies. The probability that each of these benefits will be paid depends on the worker's health and life expectancy, the likelihood of future divorce or remarriage, the number and timing of additional children, the level of future earnings, and the future work experience of the worker's spouse. For a person

8. This concept first appeared in Martin S. Feldstein, "Social Security, Induced Retirement, and Aggregate Capital Accumulation," *Journal of Political Economy*, vol. 82 (September–October 1974), pp. 905–26.

who is average in all relevant respects, the value of social security benefits is the actuarial likelihood that a randomly selected person will become eligible for one kind of benefit or another (in other words, that he or she will become disabled, live to retirement, or be survived by relatives eligible for benefits), multiplied by the benefit amount to which that person would be entitled in that contingency (which depends on the benefit formula in effect in the possibly quite distant future and earnings over that period); this amount must then be reduced to present value by discounting at a market discount rate.

Let us take for granted that this worker is willing and able to do the "correct" mental calculation to estimate his social security wealth, that he can see through the arithmetic fog brought about by inflation, and that he can effortlessly calculate all values in real terms. Such a worker must project what the social security system will look like a quarter of a century and more in the future when he expects to be retired and drawing benefits.

But how does he form such expectations? Does he expect the system to stay as it is, to shrink, or to grow? Does he anticipate structural changes? Perhaps, like many recently surveyed workers, he doubts that he will receive any retirement benefits at all. A recent study found that small differences in the ways workers form expectations about future benefits can cause differences of 50 percent in estimates of the present value of future social security retirement benefits. This study did not allow for the possibility that a sizable fraction of workers may expect no benefits at all, a fear documented in recent opinion polls.[9]

The seriousness of this problem may be dramatized by considering what expectations of future social security benefits a worker should have held who was forty years old in 1954 and expected to retire at sixty-five in 1979. (The option of receiving reduced benefits at age sixty-two did

9. Other considerations could increase the range of these uncertainties significantly. For example, much uncertainty surrounds the future course of earnings of working wives, and some surrounds the future course of real interest rates. See Dean R. Leimer and Selig Lesnoy, "Social Security and Private Saving: New Time-Series Evidence," *Journal of Political Economy*, vol. 90 (June 1982), pp. 606–42. If workers expect their initial benefits to equal 41 percent of average earnings if they are men and 25.6 percent if they are women (the values used by Martin Feldstein in the reference cited in note 8 above) and to be adjusted only for prices, the estimated social security wealth is 1.8 trillion 1972 dollars in 1977. If workers assume that the ratio of benefits to wages will stay the same as it was in 1977 and if benefits after retirement are increased at the same rate as average wages rise, then social security wealth in 1977 was $3.4 trillion.

not exist in 1954.) The system then was not indexed. Should the worker have expected no further legislative change and, if so, at what rate of inflation should he have assumed that legislated nominal benefits would be eroded? Should he have assumed that benefits would be adjusted for inflation or, perhaps, that they would be liberalized? Should he have anticipated the advent of disability insurance in 1956 or of medicare nine years later? Should he have anticipated the fears now widespread that benefits will be cut?

The point is that one must make some assumption about the answers to these questions in computing social security wealth, the principal variable used to represent social security in many recent studies of its effects on economic behavior; but the choice among plausible answers causes large variations in this key variable.

At the individual level there is great variation in all these factors. The practical impossibility of fully specifying all of them stands as a serious obstacle before effective cross-sectional analysis. Furthermore, not only must one determine the analytically correct way to make the calculation; one must also decide whether the worker really understands it.

At the aggregate level differences among people in life expectancies, health status, or marital plans can be ignored because they average out in large populations. But some problems do not go away. These include the problem of deciding how expectations are formed regarding the future course of social security law and earnings and the appropriate discount rate to assign. Thus the process by which American workers in 1970 formed expectations about the social security benefits they would receive in the future may have been rather different from those that operate today.

Despite the need for some indicator of size to measure the effect of social security on behavior, it is important to keep in mind the importance of the relatively arbitrary assumptions that must be made in order to obtain such indicators. Figure 6 shows three estimates of gross social security wealth for the United States. Two of the lines show the large differences in the estimates of gross social security wealth that result from seemingly modest technical differences in the way people are assumed to form expectations about social security benefits they will receive in the future (see the note to figure 6 for an explanation of these differences); the third line shows the consequences of an error in the program used to estimate the social security wealth that was used in

Figure 6. *Gross Social Security Wealth as a Percent of Gross National Product, 1937–74*[a]

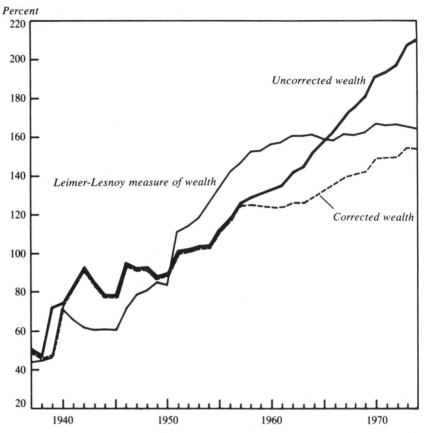

Percent

Uncorrected wealth

Leimer-Lesnoy measure of wealth

Corrected wealth

Source: Selig D. Lesnoy and Dean R. Leimer, "Social Security and Private Saving: New Time Series Evidence with Alternative Specifications," ORS Working Paper 22 (Social Security Administration, September 1981), pp. 74–77.

a. Expected social security wealth is the actuarial value of perceived future benefits expected by individuals. It is calculated as the product of the benefit ratio (benefits to personal per capita income) and the expected disposable income per capita (with a growth rate of 2 percent a year). Feldstein assumed a constant benefit ratio based on the historical average benefit ratio. Leimer and Lesnoy used the same assumptions but included more detail in the calculation of entitlement.

most time-series work before 1979.[10] Both the differences resulting from different assumptions and those stemming from the programming error are of considerable importance in assessing the reliability of available

10. The erroneous series was developed and first used by Feldstein, "Social Security, Induced Retirement, and Aggregate Capital Accumulation." The error was reported by

analyses. The central point regarding these estimates of social security wealth is not that one is right and the remainder are wrong, but rather that there is no answer that is demonstrably right and that the range of entirely plausible answers is so wide as to render the concept unusable in respectable econometric work.

Leimer and Lesnoy, "Social Security and Private Saving: A Reexamination of the Time Series Evidence Using Alternative Social Security Wealth Variables," ORS Working Paper 19 (Social Security Administration, November 1980). The error arose because Feldstein's research assistant programmed a one-time increase in benefits for widows enacted in 1956 to be repeated in every succeeding year. As a result of this error, benefits for widows were projected to grow to more than one-third of all benefits, about two times the correct value.

CHAPTER FOUR

Saving

INTEREST in the effect of social security on saving was fueled when Katona and Cagan published studies based on separate surveys suggesting that social security increases saving by bringing retirement within reach of people who otherwise would consider it unaffordable.[1] This conclusion was regarded somewhat skeptically, but relatively little econometric work was done on the effects of social security on saving until the mid-1970s, when social security emerged as the largest program in the U.S. budget.[2]

Time-Series Analysis

With his 1974 article Feldstein inaugurated a debate on whether time-series analysis of U.S. saving rates revealed any effects from the social security system.[3] Although the article was mistitled, it reported estimates of the effect of social security only on personal saving), Feldstein's presentation of the issues was characteristically lucid and his results dramatic. Social security, he reported, had reduced personal saving by half and caused the capital stock to be smaller by 38 percent because of reduced personal saving; wages had also been cut because of the smaller

1. George Katona, *The Mass Consumption Society* (McGraw-Hill, 1964), chap. 19; and Phillip Cagan, *The Effect of Pension Plans on Aggregate Saving: Evidence From a Sample Survey*, Occasional Paper 95 (Columbia University Press for the National Bureau of Economic Research, 1965).

2. Among the early exceptions were Henry Aaron, "Social Security: International Comparisons," in Otto Eckstein, ed., *Studies in Income Maintenance* (Brookings Institution, 1967); and Joseph A. Pechman, Henry J. Aaron, and Michael K. Taussig, *Social Security: Perspectives for Reform* (Brookings Institution, 1968), Appendix D, pp. 294–304.

3. Martin S. Feldstein, "Social Security, Induced Retirement, and Aggregate Capital Accumulation," *Journal of Political Economy*, vol. 82 (September–October 1974), pp. 905–26.

capital stock. There ensued a spirited scholarly debate that dealt with both Feldstein's theoretical model and his econometric methods. Now, nearly a decade later, it is clear that Feldstein's theoretical analysis has been vigorously challenged by scholars engaged in research on social security, and his empirical findings have been discredited.

According to the life-cycle model, a system of pay-as-you-go annuities will reduce saving even if people pay taxes no greater than the amounts they would willingly have saved (or if people can borrow to finance any excess of social security taxes over preferred saving).[4] Furthermore, social security has not been actuarially fair; it has provided expected benefits worth far more than taxes for all people who have received benefits to date, and it will continue to do so until the system is fully mature. On this account as well, social security should reduce personal saving.

However, social security pays benefits only after a worker has reached a certain age and only upon satisfaction of an earnings test. Feldstein pointed out that if social security induces early retirement through these provisions, it may increase desired saving because an increase in the length of retirement increases the proportion of lifetime income that cannot be consumed as earned (in other words, that must be saved) if consumption is to be sustained in retirement and if social security benefits do not cover all consumption. Thus, Feldstein argued, the combined effect of pay-as-you-go financing and the lifetime wealth increment of an immature system (which reduce saving) and the alleged inducement to early retirement (which increases saving) is theoretically indeterminant.[5]

The results of a series of regressions relating consumer expenditure to disposable income, retained earnings, per capita household wealth, retained earnings of corporations, and social security wealth indicated that each dollar of gross social security wealth decreases saving by $0.024.[6] This estimate, multiplied by the calculated amount of social security wealth and added to the direct effect of social security taxes on saving, led to an estimate that social security reduced personal saving in

4. See the section entitled "The Life-Cycle Model" in chapter 2.

5. On the issue of whether social security, in fact, induces retirement, see chapter 5.

6. Retained earnings enters the equation because households are deemed to use retained earnings as a measure of the long-term increase in the value of their stock holdings and to base their saving decisions on a plan to achieve an optimal quantity of wealth, including stock holdings.

1971 by exactly half and that the cumulative effect of such reduced saving was a reduction of 38 percent in the capital stock of the United States below what it would have been if there had been no social security system.

The major theoretical assault came from Barro, whose formulation of the multigeneration model indicated that social security, in principle, should have no effect on saving.[7] From the other side, a number of analysts have employed the finding that the elderly dissave at a much lower rate than the life-cycle model would predict or do not dissave at all to question whether the life-cycle model adopted by many analysts is a sufficiently accurate stylization of behavior to be used for empirical work.[8] Munnell argued that not all forms of personal saving, but principally those intended to support retirement (notably additions to pensions and to insurance company assets), would be affected by social security.[9]

In addition to these criticisms, several economists questioned Feldstein's econometric methods. The addition of measures of the business cycle, such as the unemployment rate, tended to reduce the estimated effect of social security on saving and to destroy its statistical significance; and the inclusion of some measure of "normal" or permanent income and of the money supply had a similar effect.[10] And, to foreshadow an issue that has been central, the estimated effect of social security on consumption and saving has been highly sensitive to the period over which the relation was estimated. In particular, the effect of social security on saving was far greater if the years from 1929 (or 1930) to 1940, as well as the postwar period starting in 1947, were included, than it was if the analysis were based only on the postwar years. Noting this peculiarity, one observer remarked, "to believe these results, one must assume that individuals in the early 1930s anticipated the coming

7. Robert J. Barro, *The Impact of Social Security on Private Saving: Evidence from the U.S. Time Series* (The American Enterprise Institute for Public Policy Research, 1978) and "Are Government Bonds Net Wealth?" *Journal of Political Economy*, vol. 84 (November–December 1974), pp. 1095–1117.

8. See chapter 2, note 22.

9. Alicia H. Munnell, "The Impact of Social Security on Personal Saving," *National Tax Journal*, vol. 27 (December 1974), pp. 553–67; and *The Effect of Social Security on Personal Saving* (Brookings Institution, 1982).

10. For a review of the debate, see Louis Esposito, "Effects of Social Security on Saving: Review of Studies Using U.S. Time Series Data," *Social Security Bulletin*, vol. 41 (May 1978), pp. 9–17; and Robert J. Barro and others, "Social Security and Private Saving: Another Look," *Social Security Bulletin*, vol. 42 (May 1979), pp. 33–40.

of social security; this would seem like an application of rational expectations with a vengeance."[11]

The coup de grace to Feldstein's original findings came from Leimer and Lesnoy, two analysts employed by the Social Security Administration, who discovered an important programming error in the construction of the estimates of social security wealth that not only Feldstein but most of his critics had used.[12] As shown in table 1, correction of this error led to estimates that social security dramatically and implausibly increased saving (see the postwar years 1947–74 in the second column),[13] or that social security had decreased saving, but by less than half as much as Feldstein had estimated (see the results including the depression years also). Other tests showed the extreme sensitivity of the results to the period of estimation. As the table indicates, dropping the years 1930 and 1931 reversed the sign of the coefficient of social security wealth and doubled its size.

Leimer and Lesnoy also pointed out that the results depend sensitively on how one assumes that people form expectations about future entitlements to social security benefits. Employing a variety of widely accepted assumptions about methods of forming expectations, they showed that one could get almost any result one sought. The third column of table 1 reports the alternative results they obtained using one of many different methods of forming expectations. Feldstein replied to their criticism by adjusting his assumptions about the formation of expectations to take account of the benefit liberalization enacted in 1972 and came up with results midway between those of Leimer and Lesnoy and his own previous results. Leimer and Lesnoy pointed out that the adjustment was one of many that might conceivably have been made; for example, taking account of the indexation of benefits after retirement, a major change enacted in 1972 but ignored by Feldstein, reduced the estimates once again.

11. Charles Upton, "Book Reviews," *The Journal of Political Economy*, vol. 83 (October 1975), p. 1092.

12. The nature of this error is described above in chapter 3, note 10 and is shown graphically in figure 6. See Dean R. Leimer and Selig Lesnoy, "Social Security and Private Saving: New Time-Series Evidence," *Journal of Political Economy*, vol. 90 (June 1982), pp. 606–42.

13. Based on the estimated coefficient for the postwar years, social security increased annual saving by $181.7 billion. Since personal saving in 1974 was only $85.1 billion, this equation implies that, but for social security, personal saving would have been a negative $96.6 billion. The *t* value on the coefficient that leads to this absurd estimate is larger than the *t* value on the coefficient in Feldstein's original equation.

Table 1. *Alternative Time-Series Estimates of the Reduction in Personal Saving per Dollar of Gross Social Security Wealth*

Period of estimation	Erroneous social security wealth	Corrected social security wealth	Actuarial perception	Feldstein adjustment
1930–71	0.024[a]	0.015[a]	n.a.	n.a.
1930–74	0.026[a]	0.011[a] (−0.003)[c]	0.001[b]	n.a.
1932–74	n.a.	−0.022[c]	n.a.	n.a.
1930–76	n.a.	0.002[a]	0.000[c]	0.014[a] (0.004)[d]
1947–71	0.014[e]	n.a.	n.a.	n.a.
1947–74	−0.019[c]	−0.061[c]	−0.004[c]	n.a.
1947–76	n.a.	n.a.	−0.004[c]	−0.022[c]

n.a. Not available.

a. Martin Feldstein, "Social Security, Induced Retirement, and Aggregate Capital Accumulation: A Correction and Update," National Bureau of Economic Research Working Paper 579, table 1.

b. Dean R. Leimer and Selig D. Lesnoy, "Social Security and Private Saving: A Reexamination of the Time Series Evidence Using Alternative Social Security Wealth Variables," ORS Working Paper 19 (Social Security Administration, November 1980).

c. Reestimation by Selig D. Lesnoy and Dean R. Leimer, "Social Security and Private Saving: New Time Series Evidence with Alternative Specifications," draft version of their "Social Security and Private Saving: New Time-Series Evidence," *Journal of Political Economy*, vol. 90 (June 1982), pp. 606–42.

d. Dean R. Leimer and Selig D. Lesnoy, "Comment," photocopied, 1981.

e. Martin S. Feldstein, "Social Security, Induced Retirement, and Aggregate Capital Accumulation," *Journal of Political Economy*, vol. 82 (September–October 1974), table 2, p. 917.

The residue of reliable findings from this debate is scant, although much has been learned about the almost infinite malleability of time-series analyses. Almost all participants have concluded that essentially nothing can be learned about the effects of social security on saving from time-series analysis. Having reviewed the available literature on the effects of transfers on saving and other forms of economic behavior, three economists concluded, "Given the reliance of most studies on the erroneous social security wealth variable, the *ad hoc* adjustments underlying Feldstein's most recent and highly variable estimates, and the careful critique and contrary results reported in Leimer-Lesnoy, we judge that there is little robust time-series evidence of a significant relationship between social security and private savings."[14] The data are insufficiently rich to enable even skilled econometricians to reach conclusions that others cannot plausibly contradict.

14. Sheldon Danziger, Robert Haveman, and Robert Plotnick, "How Income Transfer Programs Affect Work, Savings and the Income Distribution; A Critical Review," *The Journal of Economic Literature*, vol. 19 (September 1981), p. 1003.

But the problem is even more serious than that. Even the best time-series data would not suffice to produce reliable and accurate estimates. Auerbach and Kotlikoff simulated the course of consumption behavior within a model that embodied the life-cycle model by assumption. They assumed that the advent of pay-as-you-go social security would reduce saving during the transition years when early cohorts receive lifetime wealth increments.[15] They introduced an analog to social security into their model and calculated consumption, social security wealth, other wealth, and income in succeeding years. They then estimated time-series regressions of the effect of social security wealth on consumption. Despite the underlying assumption that the advent of social security would reduce saving, they obtained some estimates from these synthetic regressions that social security increased saving and some that indicated it reduced saving. Having obtained the same kind of statistical cacophony actually observed, Auerbach and Kotlikoff concluded that their results "suggest that virtually any social security time-series coefficient, negative, zero, or positive is potentially consistent with the life-cycle hypothesis."[16]

Thus it would be pointless to continue the time-series debate, even if better data should become available.

Household Cross-sectional Studies

In the search for evidence on how social security affects saving, economists have examined survey data on individual households as well as aggregate statistics. The strategy of looking at data on individual households has a major advantage over that of examining aggregate statistics, but it has an important drawback as well.

The advantage is that cross-sectional data allow strong tests of the validity of the life-cycle model on which the assertion that social security will reduce saving rests. The life-cycle model predicts that, if there are no borrowing constraints, the actuarially fair part of social security will leave consumption unaffected, reducing preretirement disposable income and saving by the same amount, and increasing postretirement

---

15. Alan J. Auerbach and Laurence J. Kotlikoff, "An Examination of Empirical Tests of Social Security and Savings," National Bureau of Economic Research, Working Paper 730, August 1981.

16. Ibid., p. 35.

disposable income and decreasing postretirement personal dissaving. This portion of social security benefits, therefore, reduces private asset holdings at all ages. It also reduces public debt dollar-for-dollar of funded social security wealth. The excess of actual benefits over the actuarially fair portion—the lifetime wealth increment—increases consumption both before and after retirement; it reduces private asset holdings because it increases consumption, but less than dollar-for-dollar of social security wealth.

Testing these predictions would be straightforward, but difficult, if adequate data were available. The ideal survey would contain detailed information on each person's ownership of assets of all kinds, including the individual's perception of accumulated rights to future social security benefits and private pensions, business ownership, equities and bonds, and on housing and other real property. It would contain detailed information on earnings histories and sufficient data on education, occupation, work experience and job tenure, and other variables to support estimates of expected future earnings. It would also contain enough information to estimate the rate at which people are prepared to trade future for present consumption (the subjective rate of time preference) for those people who are subject to capital market constraints and who cannot borrow as much as they would like at market rates of interest. It would also contain a time series of these data covering many years, so that the inevitably gradual adjustment of assets of each family to changes in its circumstances could be directly estimated.

No survey meets these standards fully. Asset data typically are skimpy, and where they are available, the other data are missing or the survey covers only a small fraction of the population. Even if all desired data were present, the problems of statistical estimation would be impressive. In one sense, the paucity of data is a blessing, as it has required analysts to adopt simple equations that are easy to understand, even if these simple equations fail to represent adequately the diversity or complexity of household characteristics or behavior.

The initial studies by Katona based on survey data collected by the Survey Research Center[17] and by Phillip Cagan of a Consumers Union survey[18] found that people with pension plans save more than those

17. Katona, *The Mass Consumption Society;* also see his *Private Pensions and Individual Saving* (University of Michigan Survey Research Center, Institute for Social Research, 1965).
18. Cagan, *The Effect of Pension Plans on Aggregate Saving.*

without such plans. The rationalization of these findings was that pensions advertised the need for income during retirement and brought retirement within reach, thereby encouraging saving by people for whom retirement would otherwise be impossible.

Little weight is now given to these studies for two reasons. First, the reanalysis of the Consumers Union data by Munnell, in which she controlled for such personal characteristics as education and age, reversed Cagan's findings.[19] Munnell found that after controlling for personal characteristics, increases in private pensions were associated with reduced holdings of other assets. Second, in an era when pension coverage was partial, one would expect that retirement- or security-oriented people in some degree would sort themselves into jobs with good pension plans.[20] Thus preferences for future consumption may have simultaneously encouraged people both to save and to acquire pension coverage.

The first, and so far the only major, cross-sectional study to find that social security reduces saving as the life-cycle model suggests, is that by Feldstein and Pellechio.[21] Based on comprehensive asset information from a sample of employed men aged fifty-five to sixty-four surveyed in 1962 and 1963 by the Federal Reserve Board, their study reported that each dollar of estimated social security wealth is associated with a reduction of roughly one dollar of other assets.[22]

Other studies find that social security reduces private asset holdings, but less than dollar-for-dollar. Kotlikoff, analyzing the longitudinal survey of males aged forty-five to fifty-nine, divided social security into its actuarially fair component and its bonus component (or lifetime

19. Munnell, *The Effect of Social Security on Personal Saving*, chap. 5.

20. One would expect this sorting out to go on also when pension plans are widespread but diverse; employees with strong preferences for saving would find jobs particularly attractive that pay a relatively large proportion of remuneration in pensions (which enjoy favored treatment under the tax system). Employees not interested in saving would tend in some degree to choose jobs with small pensions. For that reason one must be wary of cross-sectional studies of the impact of private pensions on saving or household assets. On this subject, see Alan S. Blinder, "Private Pensions and Public Pensions: Theory and Fact," paper prepared as background for the W. S. Woytinsky Lecture, delivered in Washington, D.C., December 28, 1981.

21. Martin Feldstein and Anthony Pellechio, "Social Security and Household Wealth Accumulation: New Microeconometric Evidence," *Review of Economics and Statistics*, vol. 41 (August 1979), pp. 361–68.

22. The estimated coefficient ranged from $0.51 to $1.67. But the equations explained only 8 to 26 percent of the variation in asset holdings. The equations with the best fit produced the relatively low coefficients of 0.58 and 0.69.

wealth increment).[23] He found that each dollar of the actuarially fair social security wealth reduces assets by $0.67, and each dollar of the lifetime wealth increment increases assets by $0.24.[24] These estimates are inconsistent with the life-cycle model, which suggests that the actuarially fair component should decrease assets dollar-for-dollar and that the lifetime wealth increment should decrease assets by close to that amount. The net effect was a reduction of assets by an estimated $0.13 for each dollar of social security wealth.[25] Diamond and Hausman, using the same data as Kotlikoff, found that each dollar of social security wealth is associated with a reduction of about $0.50 in other assets.[26]

Still other cross-sectional studies have found that social security has caused little or no reduction in saving or private asset holdings or has actually increased them. Kurz reports that social security has very small effects on asset holdings, positive or negative depending on the group under study and the mathematical form of the equation used in the statistical estimation.[27] Blinder, Gordon, and Wise, in perhaps the most elaborate study of the effects of pensions and social security on saving and labor supply of older men, found that people with large private pensions tend to have larger holdings of other assets (an echo of the Cagan-Katona results cited above), even after controlling for a large number of personal characteristics, and that each dollar of social security wealth is associated with a reduction of $0.39 of other assets.[28] But both

23. Laurence Kotlikoff, "Testing the Theory of Social Security and Life-Cycle Accumulation," *American Economic Review,* vol. 69 (June 1979), pp. 396–411. Data are from pp. 403–04.

24. The coefficient of the actuarially fair part is more than twice its standard error, while that of the lifetime wealth increment is barely larger than its standard error.

25. This estimate is a weighted average of the coefficient of the two components of social security benefits, with the proportion of each component in the total as weights. See Laurence J. Kotlikoff, "Testing the Theory of Social Security and Life-Cycle Accumulation," *American Economic Review,* vol. 69 (June 1979), table 2, p. 404.

26. Peter Diamond and Jerry Hausman, in "Individual Savings Behavior," a paper prepared for the National Commission on Social Security, May 1980, presented their data in different form. They found that each dollar of expected annual pension and social security income is associated with a reduction in planned wealth at age sixty-five of $5.84 and $6.93, respectively. If one assumes that life expectancy is eighteen years at age sixty-five and that the real discount rate is 3 percent, an annuity of a dollar is worth $13.75.

27. Mordecai Kurz, "The Effects of Social Security and Private Pensions on Family Savings," SRI International, April 22, 1981.

28. Alan S. Blinder, Roger H. Gordon, and Donald E. Wise, *An Empirical Study of the Effects of Pensions and Labor Supply Decisions of Older Men,* MATHTECH, March 30, 1981 and "Social Security, Bequests, and the Life-Cycle Theory of Saving: Cross-Sectional Tests," National Bureau of Economic Research, Working Paper 619, January 1981.

estimates were statistically so undependable that they could not rule out the hypotheses that private pensions had no effect on other personal savings, that social security wealth had no effect on assets, or that social security wealth reduced asset holdings dollar-for-dollar.

Numerous studies suggest that household behavior consistently contradicts a central implication of the life-cycle model: elderly people do not seem to reduce asset holdings very much after retirement and, in fact, may continue adding to them until very late ages. The evidence of Blinder, Gordon, and Wise, of Mirer, of Kurz, and of Danziger and others indicates that the elderly do not draw down assets, as the life-cycle model predicts.[29]

A second aspect of the results that casts doubt on the life-cycle model is that the estimates of the effects on saving of key variables, such as social security wealth or private pensions, consistently are much smaller than the life-cycle model predicts, or they are of the wrong sign. In addition, the inability of all models to explain more than a small fraction of the variation among households in saving and the extreme imprecision of the estimates of the effects of the key variables indicate that the life-cycle model does not correctly describe the behavior of many or most savers.

The multigeneration model fares no better. According to this model the lifetime wealth increment, a gift to the present generation at the expense of future generations, should increase bequests. No such effect is detectable from data on actual bequests, however.[30]

After concluding this survey of the results of studies based on

29. Blinder, Gordon, and Wise, *An Empirical Study of the Effects of Pensions and Labor Supply Decisions of Older Men;* Thad Mirer, "The Dissaving Behavior of the Retired Aged," *Southern Economic Journal,* vol. 46 (July 1979), pp. 1197–1205, and "The Wealth-Age Relationship among the Aged," *American Economic Review,* vol. 69 (June 1979), pp. 435–43; Kurz, "The Effects of Social Security and Private Pensions on Family Savings"; and Sheldon Danziger and others, "The Life-Cycle Hypothesis and the Consumption Behavior of the Elderly," paper prepared for the Brookings Institution Project on Research in Retirement and Aging, sponsored by the Office of Planning and Evaluation, Department of Health and Human Services. These studies report that there is relatively little dissaving of fungible wealth. There may even be net accumulation among the aged. However, the aged automatically draw down social security and pension wealth as they draw benefits and grow older. In contrast, Diamond and Hausman, using other data, report some evidence of dissaving among the aged in "Individual Savings Behavior," but less than the life-cycle model would require.

30. Martin David and Paul L. Menchik, "The Effect of Social Security on Lifetime Wealth Accumulation and Bequests," Discussion Paper 671-81 (Madison, Wisconsin: The Institute for Research on Poverty, December 1981).

household surveys, one is driven to bring the same charge against cross-sectional studies that Darby brought against time-series studies: "In conclusion, the . . . studies . . . have been unable to rule out any plausible existing beliefs on the effects of the social security program on saving."[31]

International Cross-sectional Studies

Because saving rates differ widely from one country to another, it is tempting to examine whether variations in social security benefits help explain these differences. But this method of research is plagued by particularly severe handicaps. Simple models are called upon to represent diverse cultures and institutions that generate different incentives unlikely to be captured by simple arithmetic relations. Data are collected by different methods, so that even skilled analysts may be unaware of exactly what the data mean. (See chapter 2, note 36.)

Six studies have been done in recent years, two by Feldstein that find an association between high social security benefits and low personal saving,[32] three that find no association, including one by Barro and MacDonald, which concludes agnostically, "any desired sign for the social security variable in a cross country . . . [saving] equation can be picked by judicious choice of specification . . . ,"[33] and one by Kopits

31. Michael R. Darby, "Social Security and Private Saving: Another Look," Social Security Administration, *Social Security Bulletin,* vol. 42 (GPO, May 1979), p. 36.

32. "Social Security and Private Savings: International Evidence in an Extended Life-cycle Model," in Martin S. Feldstein and Robert P. Inman, eds., *The Economics of Public Services* (Macmillan: London, 1977), pp. 174–206, and "International Differences in Social Security and Saving," *Journal of Public Economics,* vol. 14 (October 1980), pp. 225–44.

33. Erkki Koskela and Matti Virén, "Social Security and Household Saving in an International Cross Section: A Note," paper prepared by the Bank of Finland Research Department, January 28, 1982, and "A Note on Long-Term Determinants of the Private Savings Ratio, Bank of Finland Research Department, July 29, 1982. Robert J. Barro and Glenn M. MacDonald, "Social Security and Consumer Spending in an International Cross Section," *Journal of Public Economics,* vol. 11 (June 1979), pp. 275–89. The text quotation is from p. 287.

Koskela and Virén underscore the sensitivity of results to statistical methods and the choice of a sample by noting "Opposite to Feldstein's claim . . . the estimation results are not robust to the procedure of weighting observations by population size. Evidently, this is due to Austria which Feldstein later drops from his sample. Namely, switching from the weighted observations to the unweighted ones decreases the t-ratio of Feldstein's 'new retiree replacement ratio' . . . strikingly with a consequence that with the unweighted regressions we cannot even reject the hypothesis that all the coefficients of the respective equation are identically zero according to an F-test." See Koskela and Virén, "A Note on Long-Term Determinants of the Private Saving Ratio," p. 2.

and Gotur that finds that in industrial countries public pensions for the aged increase saving, that other social security benefits (notably health insurance, family allowances, unemployment insurance, work injury benefits, and aid to the indigent) reduce saving, and (oddly) that social security taxes increase saving.[34]

Summary of Evidence on Saving

For a variety of reasons, ranging from introspection and personal experience to the analysis of statistics on saving, people have developed hunches about how social security affects saving. Economists, who are no more immune to hunches than anyone else, have applied the tools of their discipline to try to determine which of these hunches is correct.

The evidence is conclusive that so far they have failed. Using the best that economic theory and statistical techniques have to offer, they have produced a series of studies that can be selectively cited by the true believers of conflicting hunches or by people with political agendas that they seek to advance.

It is appropriate at this point to take a step back from the econometric debris and to enquire why we care about how social security affects private saving. The answer, aside from intellectual curiosity, presumably stems from the belief that the nation would be better off if the capital stock were larger than it is and that we should be concerned if social security decreases personal saving. Posing the question in this way directs attention to the relevant target of policy, the capital stock. It also serves as a reminder that the capital stock results from domestic saving not only by households, but also by business and government.[35]

If our objective is to increase the rate of capital accumulation, we should ask which instruments are best for achieving that end. Prominent on the list would be direct assaults on the federal deficits, incentives to business investment, and the withdrawal of incentives that promote

34. George Kopits and Padma Gotur, "The Influence of Social Security on Household Savings: a Cross-Country Investigation," *International Monetary Fund Staff Papers*, vol. 27 (March 1980), pp. 160–90. According to estimates reported in this paper, a 1 percent increase in public pensions for the aged, other social security benefits, or social security taxes would be associated, respectively, with an increase in saving of 0.43 percent, a decrease of 0.28 percent, and an increase of 0.34 percent. See their tables 3 and 5, pp. 179 and 181.

35. Net investment by foreigners, of course, can also contribute to the domestic capital stock.

inefficient investments. We should include changes in social security benefits on that list only if we find persuasive empirical evidence that social security has had a clear effect on saving and that the effect is sufficiently large to matter, or if we find the goal of increased capital accumulation to be so important and other instruments for achieving it so deficient that we are willing to use a device of uncertain efficacy and with possibly serious side effects. In my judgment, the evidence falls grossly short of establishing the size, or even the direction, of the effects of social security on capital formation, and other instruments are numerous and practical.

If one turns to other instruments such as a reduction in the government deficit to increase national saving, it might be argued that creating a large surplus in the social security trust funds is a good way to achieve one's goal. By reducing social security benefits or boosting social security taxes (other government spending and other taxes held constant), one would add directly to national saving, if there were no offsetting effects of the kind predicted by the multigeneration model would predict.

The question that this suggestion raises is whether reductions in social security benefits or increases in the payroll tax are the ways to achieve a reduction in the government deficit that are most conducive to economic efficiency and fairness. Why should benefit reductions or payroll tax increases, rather than increases in other taxes or reductions in other government spending, be used as the instrument to raise total saving?

I conclude that the evidence does not support the position that reductions in social security benefits would be effective in increasing private saving. I conclude also that if we wish to increase capital formation, the proper objective is the total saving rate, and that raising social security payroll taxes or cutting social security benefits is a poor device for achieving that objective unless we favor them on other grounds. We should make social security policy on the basis of considerations other than its supposed effects on saving.

CHAPTER FIVE

Labor Supply

ONE of the original objectives of social security was to enable or to encourage older workers to retire without undue hardship when jobs were scarce. To achieve this goal, social security provided a pension, but the earnings test originally forced the recipient to stop essentially all work in order to get it. Despite the advent in the 1980s of the highest unemployment rates since the 1930s, concern has arisen that aspects of social security may needlessly discourage work, especially by persons in their fifties and early sixties; the fear is that these provisions boost the cost of social security and that they will reduce potential production when the economy returns to full employment. Expressing this concern, President Reagan in May 1981 proposed drastic reductions in social security that would have reduced the overall cost of the program by 23 percent. Among these proposed cuts was a reduction of up to 40 percent in benefits payable to workers who claim them before age sixty-five; this reduction was to be effective seven months later.[1]

Analysts have devoted considerable effort to discovering whether particular features of social security, or the system as a whole, discourage work, and if so, how much. They have examined the effects not only of the level of benefits and taxes, but also of such key provisions as the earnings test and actuarial adjustment. How much people want to work depends on their current net money wage, the characteristics of their job, their holdings of assets and receipt of unearned income, and a large number of personal characteristics. Social security taxes affect how

1. Specifically, for persons attaining age sixty-two, the benefit payable at that age was to be 55 percent of the benefit payable at age sixty-five rather than 80 percent. Additional changes in benefit computation would have further reduced the benefit payable at age sixty-two. The proposed abruptness of this change, together with opposition to such other provisions as reductions in disability benefits, cuts in basic benefits for all workers, and reduction in the cost-of -living adjustments, produced a political backlash that forced the president to withdraw this proposal and to appoint a commission to propose changes in social security.

much people want to work by reducing their current net money wage, and the benefit formula affects desired labor supply by increasing (or in some cases decreasing) their asset holdings and unearned income in response to additional work.

The theory of how simple taxes influence labor supply is standard and generally accepted,[2] but most taxes are complex, and the statistical problems are formidable in estimating the combined and simultaneous effects on household labor supply of the many taxes and transfer programs and the particular effects of social security.[3] Furthermore, the standard theory refers only to the number of hours worked, not to such other dimensions of labor supply as the acquisition of training, acceptance of promotion, or on-the-job effort, which may be equally important.[4]

The effect of social security taxes on current earnings is relatively straightforward. They form a wedge between gross money wages and net money wages. If workers ignore the value of accumulating entitlements to future benefits, these taxes should affect the supply of labor exactly as would any other equal change in net money wages.[5] To the extent that workers recognize the value of the accumulation of future benefits, these effects are reduced; and they vanish if the value of these accumulations exactly matches the tax. In that event, the payroll tax is not really a tax but rather a price, much as insurance premiums are the price of insurance coverage and are thought not to distort labor supply.

The effects of changes in future benefits are much harder to analyze. Because benefits will be paid in the future and only in certain contingencies and because workers are prohibited by law from borrowing against

2. See, for example, Anthony B. Atkinson and Joseph E. Stiglitz, *Lectures on Public Finance* (McGraw-Hill, 1980), pp. 23–61.

3. For a complete exposition of these difficulties, see Gary Burtless and Jerry A. Hausman, "The Effect of Taxation on Labor Supply: Evaluating the Gary Negative Income Tax Experiment," *Journal of Political Economy*, vol. 86 (December 1978), pp. 1103–30; Jerry A. Hausman, "Labor Supply," in Henry J. Aaron and Joseph A. Pechman, eds., *How Taxes Affect Economic Behavior* (Brookings Institution, 1981), pp. 27–72; Marjorie Honig and Giora Hanoch, with the collaboration of Harold Watts, "Estimation of Labor Supply and Retirement Behavior," paper prepared for the Brookings Institution Conference on Research in Retirement and Aging, sponsored by the Office of Planning and Evaluation, Department of Health and Human Services, held in Washington, D.C., January 19–30, 1981.

4. Harvey S. Rosen, "What Is Labor Supply and Do Taxes Affect It?" *American Economic Review: Papers and Proceedings*, vol. 70 (May 1980), pp. 171–81.

5. This statement assumes that changes in the payroll tax levied on employers do not affect money wages gross of all payroll taxes.

future entitlements, one must calculate the probability that each of the various kinds of benefits will be paid at specified future dates, and these amounts must be discounted to present value. The appropriate discount rate is a market rate of interest or, for people who cannot borrow as much as they want at market rates, a personal rate of time preference. Quite apart from these factors and the uncertainty about whether Congress will change the law, the effect of present earnings on the real value of benefits payable at specified future dates under particular contingencies depends on such other factors as marital status, number of minor children, and future earnings.

One must solve these problems to calculate the increase in future benefit entitlements that compensate workers for the reduction in current money income. Moreover, the solution depends on whether the life-cycle model, the multigeneration model, or the short-horizon model is the right one to use in estimating the effects of social security on labor supply. If workers heavily discount future benefits, the effects of social security will simply be those of the payroll tax; if they use market rates of discount, the effects of future entitlements may be as large as the effects of taxes or even larger.

For workers over the age of sixty-two, the effect of social security on labor supply is even more complicated, because such workers face the earnings test and actuarial adjustments of benefits.[6] The earnings test is really nothing more than a tax with a zero rate up to a certain earnings level, a 50 percent rate over a succeeding range that varies in length with the benefit entitlement, and a zero marginal rate above that level. In addition, if the earnings test comes into play, benefits will be increased in the future and the earnings history may be increased, triggering benefit recomputation. And, of course, there are federal income taxes, state and local income taxes, cash aid to the indigent under several programs, and in-kind assistance for housing, health, food, and other goods by which families may be affected. The result is a very complex tax schedule.

All these factors influence how much people want to work. But few workers are free to work exactly as long as they would prefer. Fixed costs of working make it unprofitable to work only a few hours. Employers typically require close to full-time work. Until recently, many

6. Note that because most of today's young workers someday will be over sixty-two and because labor supply decisions at different times may be interrelated, the complications introduced by the earnings test also affect currrent decisions of younger workers if they have a long planning horizon.

employers enforced mandatory retirement at certain ages or after service of a certain number of years.

What all this adds up to is that social security (as well as private pensions and other taxes and transfers) alters the distribution of money income over a worker's life. Social security simultaneously reduces money wages and confers an asset cashable later.

In general, social security may alter the labor supply of younger workers, but it is unlikely to induce them to retire.[7] In fact, one model holds that the earnings test, by imposing a high tax on earnings received after age sixty-two, induces workers to shift their labor supply from their later, highly taxed years to the years before age sixty-two, thus increasing labor supply by younger workers.[8] Older workers who want to cut back on hours often find that they must choose among continuing to work full time on their present job, taking another job that permits part-time work but offers less pay, or retiring altogether. If such workers quit their present jobs—to retire completely, to accept part-time work on another job, or to move back and forth between work and retirement—they may be eligible for a pension. Social security may affect the number of hours worked by older workers, the probability that they will claim a pension, or the probability that they will withdraw completely from the labor force, but the effect of social security hinges in part on the access of workers to other pensions, their current wages, and the wage they could earn in alternative employment.

7. The exception to this statement is disability insurance. Parsons has estimated that most of the decline in labor force participation by men aged forty-five to sixty-four is attributable to disability insurance. See Donald O. Parsons, "The Decline in Male Labor Force Participation," *Journal of Political Economy*, vol. 88 (February 1980), pp. 117–34; and "Racial Trends in Male Labor Force Participation," *American Economic Review*, vol. 70 (December 1980), pp. 911–20. However, these estimates almost certainly exaggerate the effects; see Robert H. Haveman and Barbara L. Wolfe, "The Decline in Male Labor Force Participation: Comment," who point out a number of sources of upward bias in Parson's estimates and suggest that his estimates of the elasticity of labor force participation to disability benefits is at least twenty times too large. The work by Haveman and Wolfe was supported in part by the Brookings Institution Conference on Research in Retirement and Aging, funded by the Office of Planning and Evaluation of the Department of Health and Human Services.

8. See Richard V. Burkhauser and John A. Turner, "A Time-Series Analysis on Social Security and Its Effect on the Market Work of Men at Younger Ages," *Journal of Political Economy*, vol. 86 (August 1978), pp. 701–15. But see below on whether the earnings test, combined with actuarial adjustment and benefit recomputation, constitutes a tax or a subsidy for workers aged sixty-two to sixty-five.

Because the process of retirement is so varied for different people, it is not clear how best to measure it. One can define retirement as the receipt of a pension or of social security (but then many "retirees" will be working, some full time), complete withdrawal from the labor force (but many older people who work a few hours are substantially retired, drawing pensions or social security), or employment for fewer than a stipulated number of hours (but then some involuntarily unemployed may be counted as retirees). No one of these measures of retirement is best for all purposes, and various studies have used each of them.

By simple count, most empirical studies have concluded that social security reduces labor supply of elderly workers, but the size of the estimated effects varies,[9] and some studies conclude that social security has increased labor supply or had no important effect on it.[10] All the studies have been based on household survey data.

It is hard to decide how much weight to attach to these studies in the formation of public policy, even if one puts aside the social question of

9. Several useful surveys of the effects of social security on labor supply have appeared recently. See, for example, George F. Break, "The Economic Effects of the OASI Program," in Felicity Skidmore, ed., *Social Security Financing* (MIT Press, 1981), pp. 45–81; Sheldon Danziger, Robert Haveman, and Robert Plotnick, "How Income Transfer Programs Affect Work, Saving, and the Income Distribution: A Critical Review," *The Journal of Economic Literature*, vol. 19 (September 1981) p. 1003; and Olivia S. Mitchell and Gary S. Fields, "The Effects of Pensions and Earnings on Retirement: A Review Essay," National Bureau of Economic Research Working Paper 772, September 1981."

Among the investigators who have found social security reduces labor supply are Michael J. Boskin, "Social Security and Retirement Decisions," *Economic Inquiry*, vol. 15 (January 1977), pp. 1–25; Michael J. Boskin and Michael D. Hurd, "The Effect of Social Security on Early Retirement," *Journal of Public Economics*, vol. 10 (December 1978), pp. 361–77; Joseph F. Quinn, "Microeconomic Determinants of Early Retirement: A Cross-Sectional View of White Married Men," *Journal of Human Resources*, vol. 12 (Summer 1977), pp. 329–46; Anthony J. Pellechio, "The Effect of Social Security on Retirement," National Bureau of Economic Research Working Paper 260, July 1978 and "The Social Security Earnings Test, Labor Supply Distortions and Foregone Payroll Tax Revenue," National Bureau of Economic Research Working Paper 272, August 1978; and Richard V. Burkhauser, "The Early Acceptance of Social Security: An Asset Maximization Approach," *Industrial and Labor Relations Review*, vol. 33 (July 1980), pp. 484–92.

10. See Cordelia Katherine Wagner Reimers, "The Timing of Retirement of American Men" (Ph.D. dissertation, Columbia University, 1977); Laurence J. Kotlikoff, "Testing the Theory of Social Security and Life-Cycle Capital Accumulation," *American Economic Review*, vol. 69 (June 1979), pp. 396–411; Roger H. Gordon and Alan S. Blinder, "Market Wages, Reservation Wages, and Retirement Decisions," *Journal of Public Economics*, vol. 14 (October 1980), pp. 277–308; and Richard V. Burkhauser and John A. Turner, "A Time Series Analysis of Social Security and Its Effect on the Market Work of Men at Younger Ages," *Journal of Political Economy*, vol. 86 (August 1978), pp. 701–15.

whether older workers should be encouraged to retire.[11] First, because of inadequacies in the data none of the studies correctly specifies the way in which social security and other variables interact to influence labor supply. The shortcomings are not perfectionist quibbles with which analysts like to deflate the work of competitors but fundamental inadequacies that, as indicated below, undermine the believability of the results. Second, many of the studies refer to the global effects of the social security system, not to provisions that are likely to be changed. A few studies focus on such provisions of the system as the earnings test; these studies are examined more closely below.

Fundamental Structure

Among the factors that influence decisions by older workers on whether to leave their present job or to retire completely other than such personal considerations as health and asset holdings, several stand out as relevant and important.[12] The present and future amount of net wages on the current job, of net wages that could be earned in alternative employment, and of net private pension benefits and contributions and net social security benefits and payroll taxes. The values of all of these variables are contingent on the date of retirement.[13] After a careful review of empirical research, Mitchell and Fields point out: "To date, no empirical study takes into account the current values of all six

11. Once again, this issue hinges on the model that one feels best represents the behavior of typical households. If people, in fact, make lifetime plans rationally on the basis of the best available information, it can be argued that one should strive through public policy not to interfere with or to alter these plans. Even in such a case, there is a place for mandatory social security systems, for example, to protect people against the consequences of protracted economic slack, a contingency against which individuals are powerless to insure themselves. See Peter A. Diamond, "A Framework for Social Security Analysis," *Journal of Public Economics,* vol. 8 (December 1977), pp. 275–98. But if people are myopic in their plans, so that in general they reach retirement ages with fewer assets than they would have chosen if they had correctly appraised when young their preferences and resources when old, it is arguable that social security should promote retirement. But this issue is fundamentally insoluble and, as suggested above, is put to one side here and in all empirical studies.

12. See Mitchell and Fields, "The Effects of Pensions and Earnings on Retirement."

13. For example, deferring one's claim of a social security benefit beyond age sixty-two reduces the period during which benefits are received but increases each payment. In contrast, deferring a private pension after eligibility shortens the period of payment but does not increase each payment for the 65 percent of all people covered by private pensions who have defined-benefit plans.

variables, let alone their streams over time" and conclude "that most of the empirical studies do not tell us much about the effects of wage and pension streams on retirement behavior."[14]

The best way to formulate the worker's decision on whether or not to retire depends on how farsighted one takes workers to be. Most analysts of the effects of social security on labor supply begin with some form of the life-cycle model, but the lack of data forces them to adopt specifications of behavior not wholly consistent with the theory. The central problem is that the life-cycle model postulates that workers base their labor supply (and saving) not just on current earnings or pensions, but on the present discounted value of expected future income from all sources. Such data are never available. As a result, different investigators have used a variety of measures not only of retirement, but also of social security benefits, wage rates, and private pensions.[15]

That these choices are not simply matters of statistical convenience, but bear importantly on the results, is demonstrated starkly by one study with data sufficiently rich to permit the authors to use alternative measures of these key variables; Fields and Mitchell measured in four different ways the effect of social security on the age of retirement of a sample of 390 workers, three of which are used in various other studies. They found that these variations produced estimates that social security delayed retirement, accelerated it, or left it substantially unchanged, all for the same sample of workers and the same data.[16]

14. Mitchell and Fields, "The Effects of Pensions and Earnings on Retirement," pp. 41, 45.

15. Social security has been measured by social security wealth (its current value, its value two years ago, its value in a fixed year, its ratio to income, and minus past and future taxes), dummy variables for eligibility, and current reported benefits.

Earnings have been measured as gross actual earnings for active workers and estimated imputed earnings for those who are not, hourly wage rates (both gross and net of payroll taxes), present value of expected earnings until age sixty-five (or sixty-seven), change in wages between two years, one of four hourly wage brackets, and gross wages plus increase in the present value of social security entitlements. None of these measures is correct, as total compensation after taxes, including both money earnings and fringe benefits, should be used. No large cross-sectional survey has accurate data on total compensation.

Pensions have been measured by gross annual benefits, industry dummy variables, eligibility dummy variables, or the present value of expected benefits.

16. Gary S. Fields and Olivia S. Mitchell, "Economic Determinants of the Optimal Retirement Age; An Empirical Investigation," National Bureau of Economic Research Working Paper 876, April 1982. Using their preferred specification, their estimates yield the prediction that a 10 percent increase in the social security benefits payable at each age (which raises both lifetime wealth and the incremental benefit for each additional year of

The weakness of the data and the problems and importance of specification, together with the theoretical indeterminacy of the expected effects, weaken the reliance one can place on past studies of the effects of social security as a whole on labor supply. About all that can be said is that the preponderance of a series of studies, whose evidentiary value is quite low, suggests that social security as a whole diminishes the labor supply of elderly workers by some amount. This conclusion does not take one any farther than a naive perusal of the trends shown in figures 4 and 5.[17]

Specific Aspects of Social Security

Few people now propose drastic immediate reductions or increases in the overall size of the social security system, although some would sharply curtail its future rate of growth and a few would increase it. But many would change particular features of the system, notably the payment of retirement benefits before age sixty-five, the payment of "full" benefits as early as sixty-five, and the application of the earnings test to beneficiaries. Because these proposals are receiving serious consideration, studies that shed some light on their likely effects deserve close scrutiny.

Early Retirement

The proposal by President Reagan in May 1981 to curtail benefits paid to people who claim them before age sixty-five was the administration's response to the growing public doubt about the wisdom of paying benefits that appear to encourage early retirement. In addition, there has been widespread discussion of other proposals to decrease benefits payable at later ages as well.[18]

---

work) would delay retirement about eight months for the average worker in their sample. An increase of 10 percent in the present value of social security benefits, but with no change in the incremental benefit, will hasten retirement by about four months. Clearly the substitution effect outweighs the income effect, according to their estimates.

17. The prospects that future research can improve understanding of the effects of social security on labor supply are better than hopes for improving our understanding of its effects on saving because existing surveys come closer to being adequate for the analysis of labor supply.

18. The 1979 Advisory Council on Social Security by a narrow margin urged Congress

Figure 7. *Proportion of Cohorts Reaching Age Sixty-two That Claimed Early Retirement Benefits by Ages Sixty-two, Sixty-three, and Sixty-four, 1961–75*

Percent (cumulative)

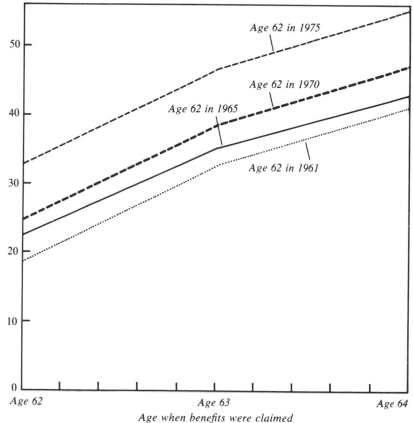

Age when benefits were claimed

Source: *Social Security Bulletin, Annual Statistical Supplement, 1980,* table 65, p. 123.

Most start receiving benefits before age sixty-five, and the proportion has been increasing (see figure 7). The question is, why is the proportion of workers claiming benefits before age sixty-five increasing? There are at least three competing explanations.

---

to examine a proposed change that would pay benefits as large as those provided under current law only to workers sixty-eight or older. Benefits for all people who claim benefits at an earlier age would be reduced under the council's plan. See *Report of the 1979 Advisory Council on Social Security* (GPO, 1980), pp. 175–77.

First, the cause might lie wholly outside the social security system. As incomes rise, people consume more of many goods including leisure. Thus the growing tendency of workers to claim benefits before age sixty-five might be attributable to rising incomes. It is conceivable that older workers are sicker or that the labor market is more hostile to older workers than in the past. Evidence in support of either proposition is lacking. Or the spread of private pensions could encourage early retirement. Both the availability of private pensions and the fact that most are not increased if one continues to work after eligibility is attained might have this effect.

Second, social security might encourage early retirement if it paid people more over their lifetimes if benefits were claimed sooner than later. Although early retirement does not increase expected lifetime benefits, on the average, it does so for some workers, particularly those with an old spouse or a short life expectancy.

Third, the financial incentives of social security might be neutral, but people might misperceive the value of the streams of benefits payable at age sixty-two and at age sixty-five and irrationally favor the former over the latter. For example, if the planning horizon of the typical older worker were shorter than the life-cycle model implies, the immediate payment of benefits at age sixty-two might appear more attractive than an objectively equivalent stream of larger payments begun three years later. Which one, or more, of these factors is at work?

The answer is disturbingly fuzzy. Incomes have been rising for a long time, and the trend of older workers to withdraw from the labor force predates social security (see figures 4 and 5). But there are no very good estimates of how far this explanation goes. Social security probably creates incentives for people to retire at age sixty-five, but it may actually encourage work between sixty-two and sixty-five, if one uses the life-cycle framework for analysis. As noted above, social security benefits payable on a given earnings history are increased for each year that workers defer claiming them. This "actuarial" adjustment, on the average, almost exactly compensates workers between ages sixty-two and sixty-five for the deferral of payments.[19] But it insufficiently com-

19. See chapter 1, note 8 above for the details of the adjustment. The phrase "on the average" is crucial. A single male of sixty-two has a life expectancy of about sixteen years and can expect to receive benefits for that period. On the average, at least one member of a couple consisting of a man age sixty-two and a spouse ten years younger can expect to receive benefits for 28.1 years. Clearly the same adjustment for deferring receipt of benefits

pensates people who continue working past age sixty-five for the deferral of payments.

If this adjustment were the only one made, one would conclude that social security is neutral in its effects on the decision by workers aged sixty-two to sixty-five about whether or not to retire and that it promotes retirement by older workers. In addition, however, extra work increases lifetime earnings and may increase the basic benefit, quite apart from the actuarial adjustment. Blinder, Gordon, and Wise claim that this recomputation of average earnings, combined with actuarial adjustment, results in what amounts to a wage subsidy for continued work by persons aged sixty-two to sixty-five; that is, an additional year of work does not decrease, but in fact increases, the present discounted value of social security benefits, and by more than the additional payroll taxes the worker will pay.[20] If one's empirical estimates lead one to predict that a higher wage rate will increase labor supply (recall that the effect in theory is indeterminate, and empirical estimates suggest that wage increases raise slightly the labor supply of nonaged males), social security encourages workers aged sixty-two to sixty-four to continue working and older workers to retire.[21]

If social security provides a bonus to continued work between the ages of sixty-two and sixty-five, if higher wages increase labor supply, and if workers understand these incentives and make plans as the life-cycle model suggests, one would expect to see few benefit claims at ages sixty-two through sixty-four (except by those who have become too sick to continue working or by those who cannot find work and exhaust unemployment benefits) and a cluster at age sixty-five. The pattern of figure 7 indicates that although benefit claims peak at age sixty-five, a

---

by one year is not appropriate in both cases. But limits to administrative capabilities prevent precise calculations in each case.

20. See Alan S. Blinder, Roger H. Gordon, and Donald E. Wise, "Rhetoric and Reality in Social Security Analysis—A Rejoinder," *National Tax Journal*, vol. 34 (December 1981), p. 475. They estimate that for married workers who reached age sixty-two in 1972 social security constituted a 35.9 percent wage subsidy over their next three years. For single men the subsidy was only 4.1 percent. Even for workers over age sixty-five, they find that automatic benefit recomputation substantially offsets the inadequacy of the actuarial adjustment, producing a 10 percent wage subsidy for married workers and a 29 percent tax on single men.

21. Richard V. Burkhauser and John A. Turner challenge the validity of the calculations by Blinder, Gordon, and Wise in "Can Twenty-five Million Americans Be Wrong?—A Response to Blinder, Gordon, and Wise," *National Tax Journal*, vol. 34 (December 1981), pp. 467–72. For a reply, see Blinder, Gordon, and Wise, "Rhetoric and Reality in Social Security Analysis—A Rejoinder."

large and increasing number of claims is occurring during the three preceding years.

The increasing tendency to claim benefits before age sixty-five might reflect the growing average wealth of later cohorts. It might signify either a drastic decline in the health or work opportunities for persons aged sixty-two through sixty-four, but there is no evidence for either trend. Alternatively, it contradicts either the assumption that labor supply increases with higher wages or the assumption that people understand social security's incentives. If people fully understand the incentives of the social security system, the trend toward early retirement is traceable either to a strong tendency for work effort to decline as wages increase (for which there is no empirical support) or to forces outside the social security system. But the likelihood that people understand the complexities of benefit recomputation and actuarial adjustment is small. If analysts failed until recently to unravel their effects and continue to disagree about whether they constitute a subsidy or a tax, how likely is it that workers and their spouses can find the answer?

While this puzzle is intriguing and relevant to the question of the overall effect of social security on labor supply and of the earnings test in particular, it is irrelevant to the observer who is persuaded on some basis that people retire too early (or too late) and should be encouraged to work more (or less). For such observers it is sufficient to know that empirical evidence suggests that some changes in social security would encourage workers to defer or accelerate retirement. Available empirical research suggests that reducing or denying benefits paid to people who retire early will discourage early retirement, and the effect will be strengthened if later benefits are sustained or if the importance in the computation of benefits of earnings received just before retirement is increased.[22]

The Earnings Test

The payment of benefits only to people who have low current earnings has been a basic principle of the social security system since its creation. This principle is expressed in the earnings test, which has been the most unpopular aspect of the system. Each year dozens of members of Congress sponsor bills to repeal it. Periodically Congress responds to

22. As an extreme, if absurd, example, payment of benefits based only on earnings received in the sixty-fourth year would powerfully discourage retirement by workers who are sixty-four years old.

this pressure by raising the amount that can be earned without loss of benefits, but so far it has resisted pressures to lift the ceiling altogether.

If benefits were paid only to those who meet the requirements of the earnings test but were increased enough to compensate workers fully for the deferral, the long-run cost would be the same as repeal of the earnings test. For this reason it is sometimes said that removing the earnings ceiling or full actuarial adjustment of benefits for deferral are alternative ways of repealing the earnings test. However, the distribution of benefits among people and over time would differ; for example, people who never retire would fare very differently under these two changes unless a large lump-sum payment to the worker's estate were made at his death.

The resistance to either of these changes has rested on three arguments. The first holds that there is little social value in paying annuities to people who continue to have earnings and, hence, have less need for external financial support than do those who have retired. The second stresses that the majority of the cost of removing the earnings test would be incurred on behalf of workers with relatively high earnings, whose needs are less pressing than those of other groups that might be served with limited federal revenues. The third rests on the fact that removing the earnings test will increase benefits immediately; and real short-run budgetary pressures always seem to prevail over abstract distaste for the denial of some or all benefits on account of current earnings.

In fact, as noted above, the earnings test is fully offset for workers under age sixty-five and partly offset for workers over that age by the fact that benefits are increased by deferral of payments. It is doubtful, however, whether people understand actuarial adjustment and benefit recomputation as well as they understand the earnings test; and for this reason the effects on behavior may be rather different from what they would be if the financial implications of all provisions were transparent. There is some evidence that the earnings test reduces the labor supply of older workers,[23] but there is none on the effects of actuarial adjustment. Part of the uncertainty arises from evasion of the earnings test to an unknown, but possibly important, degree. It is not known, therefore, whether full actuarial adjustment, which has the same long-run financial implications as removing the earnings test, would produce similar effects on labor supply.

23. Anthony Pellechio, "The Social Security Earnings Test, Labor Supply Distortions and Foregone Payroll Tax Revenue," Working Paper 272 (National Bureau of Economic Research, August 1978).

Summary of Evidence on Labor Supply

With labor supply, as with saving, one should step back and ask why we care about the effect of social security. Once again, the reason must be that we feel, for one reason or another, that American workers, especially older workers, should work more than they do. If we are persuaded that incentives should be changed to encourage later retirement, the relevant question for policymakers is not whether social security as a whole has encouraged or discouraged retirement, but which of the multiplicity of influences, economic and social, that influence retirement decisions should be altered. The answer depends not only on the effects of social security, but also on those of private pensions, general labor policy, and controllable labor market conditions.

If we conclude that the retirement age should be changed, empirical research tells us that social security may be one among many instruments for altering it, but it now gives us little indication of the size of the response we can expect. The prospects for improving our estimates of the effects of social security on labor supply are good, in contrast to the dismal prospects of making significant improvements with respect to saving. But it will be several years before we discover whether those prospects are realized. Meanwhile, if we are determined to promote work by older workers we should consider, along with such modifications in social security as changes in the age at which benefits are made available, alterations in laws under which private pensions are regulated (for example, to require the actuarial adjustment of private pensions if payment is deferred), or tax laws governing tax-sheltered savings (for example, to prohibit withdrawals from independent retirement accounts and Keogh plans as early as age fifty-nine and a half), and other policies to alter demand for workers of different ages. We should also be aware of the fact that changes which reward continued work seem to be at least as effective in encouraging work as the denial of benefits at an early age.[24]

24. The results of the study by Fields and Mitchell cited in chapter 5, note 16, for instance, call to mind the possibility of a costless swap of reduced early benefits for increased later benefits, both elements of which would boost labor supply.

CHAPTER SIX

Income Distribution

IN the course of collecting $154 billion in payroll taxes from 115 million workers and paying $160 billion in cash benefits to 36 million beneficiaries in 1982, the social security system is bound to change the distribution of income perceptibly. Having read the preceding chapters, no one should be surprised to learn that there are different ways of interpreting the data on the distributional effects of social security and that these differences are related to the three models sketched at the beginning of this book.

Alternative Frameworks

As its name indicates, the life-cycle model suggests that social security alters the distribution of income by paying benefits that are worth more or less than the taxes recipients pay over their entire lives. Benefits and taxes must be discounted to a particular date; and in this process the choice of one discount rate rather than another will have an important effect on the results, as will be apparent below. It is possible for entire cohorts to receive more or less in benefits than they have paid in taxes. Within age cohorts, particular groups, defined by earnings, family status, sex, or other characteristics, may receive benefits worth more or less than they have paid in taxes.

Within the framework of the multigeneration model, social security has all the effects to which the life-cycle model draws attention, and one feature that cancels out many of these effects. To the extent that today's beneficiaries receive more (or less) than they have paid in taxes, they bequeath a liability (or an asset) to subsequent generations. Because each generation takes such liabilities or assets into account in assessing its own well-being, it will take steps, according to the multigeneration model, to offset the effects of these transfers on subsequent generations. Thus if social security affected all members of a given cohort identically and everyone responded similarly to it, the apparent effects on distribution would be illusory because they would exclude the actions that people took to offset them.

Social security obviously does not affect all members of a given cohort identically, and various people behave in different ways. Furthermore, it is impossible in practice for particular people to identify what proportion of the difference between benefits received and taxes paid by their cohort would redound to the benefit or harm of their heirs.

Within the short-horizon model, one focuses on how social security benefits and taxes change disposable incomes measured over relatively brief periods of time, a year or perhaps longer. Payroll taxes are viewed as reducing disposable income of covered workers now, and little attention is paid to the accumulation of subsequent benefits as an offset. Beneficiaries receive increases in disposable income; previous taxes are not balanced currently against them.

During the subsequent review of data on the economic status of the aged and of the effects of social security on that status, it is important to keep in mind that particular statistics may or may not provide useful information, depending on the model within which they are viewed.

The Economic Status of the Aged

Although the aged are viewed as economically disadvantaged, the fact is that they are about as well off financially today as the nonaged. A variety of statistics support this assertion.

As shown in figure 8, the proportion of the aged with money incomes below officially designated poverty thresholds is negligibly higher than the proportion of the entire population. This similarity emerged in the late 1970s. If one takes into account benefits in kind, then slightly fewer of the aged than nonaged may fall below official poverty thresholds.[1]

1. See Timothy M. Smeeding, *Alternative Methods for Valuing Selected In-kind Transfer Benefits and Measuring Their Effect on Poverty,* Technical Paper 50 (U.S. Department of Commerce, Bureau of the Census, March 1982), table F-1, pp. 142–44, and G. William Hoagland, "The Effectiveness of Current Transfer Programs in Reducing Poverty," paper presented at Middlebury College Conference on Economic Issues, "Welfare Reform: Goals and Realities," April 19, 1980. Based on concepts slightly different from those used in compiling the data for figure 8, Smeeding estimated that the fractions of the nonelderly and elderly who were poor, using money income in 1979, were 10.6 percent and 14.7 percent, respectively. If selected in-kind benefits other than medical

Figure 8. *Percent of the Population below the Official Poverty Threshold, 1959–81*

Percent

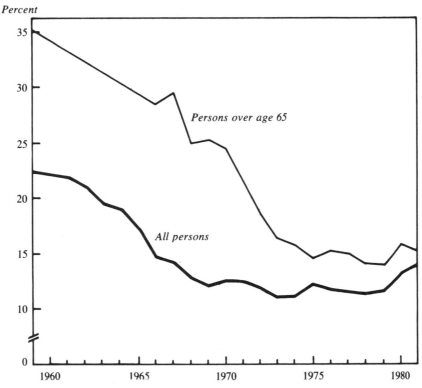

Source: U.S. Bureau of the Census, *Current Population Reports: Consumer Income, Characteristics of the Population below the Poverty Level: 1979*, Series P-60, No. 130, p. 3.

If the average income of the elderly is compared with that of the general population, the result is somewhat confusing. The average income of elderly households is just over half as large as that of households in general. Because elderly households are relatively small, however, per capita income of the elderly is slightly higher than that of

care are valued at market price, the proportions, respectively, are 8.9 percent and 12.9 percent; if medical benefits are included, the proportions are 6.7 percent and 4.5 percent. If selected in-kind benefits other than medical care are valued at an estimate of their cash equivalent value to recipients, the proportions are 9.0 percent and 13.1 percent; if medical benefits are included, the proportions are 8.2 percent and 8.0 percent. Hoagland reached similar results based on his analysis, originally performed for the Congressional Budget Office. See "Poverty Status of Families under Alternative Definitions of Income (CBO, 1977).

the general population.[2] This statistic ignores two offsetting factors. Because of economies of scale, small households require more income per capita than do large households to achieve an equivalent standard of living. The per capita poverty threshold for a family of four persons, for example, is 78 percent of that of a couple and 50 percent of that of an unrelated individual. Because the aged live predominantly in one- and two-person families, they would require more income per capita on this account to achieve the same standard of living as the nonaged. On the other hand, the aged are more likely than the nonaged to have completely paid for and to own such consumer durables as houses and automobiles, thus enabling them to achieve a living standard equivalent to that of the nonaged with about 15 percent less income.[3]

These findings suggest that the elderly on the average are able to sustain consumption during retirement about equal to the average consumption they could achieve over their lifetime. A study based on survey data supports this inference. Kotlikoff and others estimate that more than 80 percent of the members of a representative sample of older workers will have the resources to consume at the same rate during retirement as they could before retirement; and more than 95 percent will be able to sustain at least 80 percent of average lifetime consumption.[4] This conclusion rests on the willingness of the elderly to act according to the life-cycle model. If, as numerous studies suggest, the elderly are unwilling to consume as much as the life-cycle model dictates, actual consumption may fall well below potential. The policy implications of such behavior are far from clear.

Social security is the largest single source of income for the elderly. In 1978 social security provided 39 percent of the total money income of the elderly, but 76 percent of the income of the elderly poor.[5] The ratio of the average social security benefit to the official poverty threshold for

2. See Michael Hurd and John B. Shoven, "Real Income and Wealth of the Elderly," *The American Economic Review*, vol. 72 (May 1982, *Papers and Proceedings, 1981*), p. 315. In 1978 the ratio of per household income of the elderly to per household income of the entire population was 0.58; the ratio of per capita incomes was 1.06.

3. Jacques van der Gaag and others, "From Consumer Expenditures to Consumption," progress report for the Brookings Institution Project on Research in Retirement and Aging, funded by the Office of Planning and Evaluation, Department of Health and Human Services, Washington, D.C., August 1981.

4. See Laurence J. Kotlikoff, Avia Spivak, and Lawrence H. Summers, "The Adequacy of Savings," August 1980.

5. Social Security Administration, *Social Security Bulletin, Annual Statistical Supplement, 1980* (Government Printing Office, 1980), table 8, p. 62.

Figure 9. *Average Social Security Benefits as a Percent of the Official Poverty Threshold for Aged Couples, 1959–81*

Percent

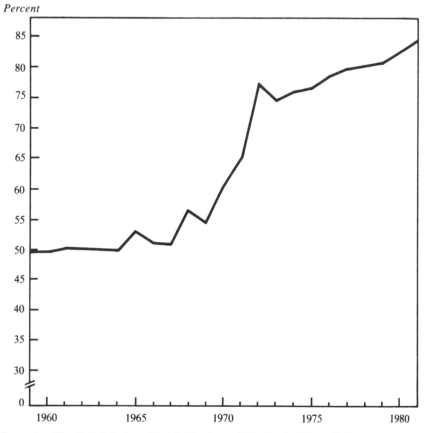

Source: *Social Security Bulletin, Annual Statistical Supplement, 1980,* tables 7 and 16, pp. 60, 71.

an aged couple has risen from 0.496 in 1959 to 0.604 in 1970 and to 0.842 in 1981 (see figure 9). It is apparent that social security has contributed to the economic gains of the aged, as measured by the decline in the proportion of poor.

These aggregate statistics in no way contradict the assertion that particular groups among the aged—widows or the very old, for example—have below-average income and above-average rates of poverty. In much the same sense and for similar reasons, some groups among the nonaged—families with female heads of household, for example—have lower than average incomes and higher than average rates of poverty.

These statistics do suggest that the combination of income sources now available to the elderly suffices to prevent them from having lower incomes on the average than do the nonelderly and to prevent real consumption opportunities from declining at retirement.

Effects on the Life-Cycle Distribution of Income

All the foregoing statistics, except the estimates of sustainable consumption by Kotlikoff and others, refer to annual income measures. They implicitly rest on the view that social security is a tax-transfer system and that these short-term tax-transfer effects deserve primary attention.[6] None of them tells anything about the life-cycle effects of social security on the distribution of income. In particular, they do not reveal whether social security has provided particular cohorts or other groups with benefits worth more or less than the taxes they have paid.

To measure such effects, one must look at the payroll taxes paid and the benefits typical workers receive over their lives. When people enter the labor force, they expect to pay taxes for an extended period and subsequently to receive benefits. Because older workers face a briefer tax-paying period before they retire than do younger workers and can expect to receive most of their benefits in the more immediate future than can younger workers, older workers have accumulated an asset, social security wealth, the excess of the present value of future benefits over future taxes. At any given time this asset is not only large relative to other forms of wealth but also distributed far more evenly than are other forms of fungible wealth.[7]

Such calculations have little meaning within the life-cycle framework,

6. See Joseph A. Pechman, Henry J. Aaron, and Michael K. Taussig, *Social Security: Perspectives for Reform* (Brookings Institution, 1968), Appendix D, pp. 294–304.

7. Martin Feldstein, "Social Security and the Distribution of Wealth," *Journal of the American Statistical Association*, vol. 71 (December 1976), pp. 800–07. Among families with male heads aged thirty-five to sixty-four in 1962, social security wealth was greater than all fungible wealth combined for the 82 percent of families with fungible wealth of less than $25,000 in 1962 dollars. These groups owned only 24.4 percent of fungible wealth, but 73.7 percent of the social security wealth. In contrast, the class with net fungible wealth of $250,000 or more included only 0.9 percent of the population, owned 28.1 percent of the fungible wealth, but only 1.2 percent of the social security wealth. More up-to-date estimates of social security wealth by income class are reported in Martin Feldstein and Anthony Pellechio, "Social Security Wealth: The Impact of Alternative Inflation Adjustments," *Policy Analysis with Social Security Research Files*, Research Report 52 (Social Security Administration, 1978), pp. 693–714.

however. In that context, the relevant question is how the present value of *all* social security taxes expected to be paid during the worker's entire lifetime relates to the present value of all expected social security benefits. Many estimates of the difference between these two quantities have been made. Although the methods vary and some findings remain in dispute, other conclusions are beyond question.

Cohort Effects

It is clear, for example, that all cohorts who have reached retirement age to date have received benefits worth far more than the taxes they have paid, if one uses plausible discount rates.[8] Moreover, the absolute size of the net gain has been increasing, so that the largest gains have been enjoyed by cohorts retiring most recently. These gains reflect the fact that the first monthly social security benefits were paid only three years after the first payroll taxes were collected and in amounts far greater than taxes paid could actuarially justify. They reflect, in addition, the continued liberalization of social security, notably the large increases in benefits enacted in 1950 and again in the early 1970s.

The internal rate of return—the discount rate that would just equate benefits with the sum of employer and employee taxes—has been declining since the early 1950s, however, from a high of about 20 percent to 8.5 percent in 1977; this rate will continue to decline.[9] Burkhauser and Warlick have calculated the lifetime wealth increment for various cohorts

8. Based on Robert Moffitt, "Trends in Social Security Wealth by Cohort," paper prepared for the National Bureau of Economic Research Conference on Income and Wealth, Madison, Wisconsin, May 14–15, 1982. Moffitt uses a 3 percent real discount rate, but shows that the use of a discount rate of 2 percent or 4 percent does not affect the results.

9. Alan Freiden, Dean Leimer, and Ronald Hoffman did detailed calculations based on actual earnings histories for the cohorts reaching retirement age in the years 1967 through 1970 in *Internal Rates of Return to Retired Worker-Only Beneficiaries under Social Security, 1967–70*, Studies in Income Distribution, no. 5 (U.S. Department of Health, Education, and Welfare, October 1976). During these four years the internal rates of return for men were 13.18 percent, 12.14 percent, 10.95 percent, and 10.61 percent. For women, the rates were 19.25 percent, 18.57 percent, 16.97 percent, and 15.74 percent.

The apparent inconsistency between the fact that the excess of benefits over taxes at a discount rate of roughly 3 percent has been rising and the fact that the internal rate of return has been falling is easily reconciled. These two facts indicate that the absolute value of benefits, calculated at a discount rate of 3 percent, has been rising faster than the absolute value of taxes at the same discount rate; but taxes have been rising at a faster rate than benefits from a smaller base.

and, within cohorts, for various earnings brackets. They find that the absolute value of the lifetime wealth increment was larger in 1972 for older retirees than for younger retirees, and that it was roughly proportional across earnings classes.[10]

How far the rate of return declines depends on future legislative action, demographic trends, and economic developments. All cohorts reaching retirement (although not necessarily all workers within each cohort) will continue for the next seventy-five years to receive positive internal rates of return under all demographic and economic assumptions used by the Social Security Administration actuaries if present law regarding benefits is not changed, and payroll taxes are changed so that revenues match benefits each year (in other words, if taxes are changed so that all annual deficits and surpluses are eliminated). In a forthcoming study, using economic assumptions more pessimistic than those used by the Social Security Administration actuaries in their intermediate forecasts, Russell finds that the real internal rate of return for workers who reach age sixty-five will range from 2.6 to 4.9 percent for cohorts entering the labor force from 1960 to 2000.[11] Using slightly different assumptions, Leimer and Petri calculated real internal rates of return for workers at age twenty-two ranging from 3.7 percent for workers who entered the labor force in 1960 to 2.5 percent for workers entering in 2000.[12] To date all workers, whatever their earnings levels or marital status at retirement, have received large positive rates of return.[13]

These results seem to contradict widely reported findings of other

10. Richard V. Burkhauser and Jennifer L. Warlick, "Disentangling the Annuity from the Redistributive Aspects of Social Security in the United States," *The Review of Income and Wealth*, vol. 27 (April 1981), pp. 401–21.

11. Louise Russell, *The Baby Boom Generation and the Economy* (Brookings Institution, 1982), pp. 153–58. Russell calculated the internal rate of return to cohorts entering the labor force from 1960 to 2000. She made nine estimates for each cohort based on the Social Security Administration actuaries' 1979 optimistic, intermediate, and pessimistic assumptions regarding all variables other than real wage growth and assumed rates of growth of real wages of 0, 1.0, and 2.0 percent. The estimates reported in the text assume a 1.0 percent rate of growth of real wages. Workers entering the labor force in 1970 will enjoy a real rate of return, according to Russell's estimates, of 3.0 to 4.6 percent, depending on the choice of economic and demographic assumptions. Those entering in 2000 will enjoy a real rate of return of 1.1 to 3.9 percent.

12. Dean R. Leimer and Peter A. Petri, "Cohort Specific Effects of Social Security Policy," *National Tax Journal*, vol. 34 (March 1981), pp. 9–28. Leimer and Petri assume that growth of real wages is 1.75 percent, but their estimates are lower than Russell's. Their estimates consider all net transfers of old age and survivors insurance and allow for mortality before age sixty-five; Russell does not.

13. See *Report of the 1979 Advisory Council on Social Security* (GPO, 1980), p. 61.

scholars that young workers now in the labor force and future entrants will receive social security benefits worth much less than the payroll taxes they and their employers are now being forced to pay.[14] These studies report estimates of the present value of social security benefits and taxes based on an assumed real discount rate of 3 percent. They present estimates that the net benefits enjoyed by current retirees will be unavailable to future retirees who have spent all or most of their working lives paying taxes necessary over the long-run to support the systems under which they will receive benefits. On the contrary, they estimate that young workers will receive benefits worth less than the taxes they will pay.

How should one interpret these apparently conflicting results? Will social security yield positive rates of return for the indefinite future, or is it saddling young workers with taxes they will never fully recover in benefits?

At a purely formal level, there is no necessary conflict. If the estimated internal rate of return is below the discount rate assumed in the calculations of present discounted value, it is possible for both sets of findings to be valid. The calculation of present value simply reports that money invested at a higher rate of return (the 3 percent assumed discount rate, for example) would accumulate to a larger sum than it would at the rate implicit in social security (say, 2 percent).[15] Unless it can be shown that the assumed discount rate (say, 3 percent) is, in some sense, the "right" rate or a minimum target, the calculations of present discounted value have no legitimate significance.

In approaching this question, it is important to keep in mind that the range of benefits that social security offers cannot be replicated now in the private sector because no package of private benefits is fully indexed against inflation. It has been shown that a judicious selection of private

14. See, for example, Michael J. Boskin, Marcy Avrin, and Kenneth Cone, "Modelling Alternative Solutions to the Long-Run Social Security Funding Problem," paper presented to the National Bureau of Economic Research Conference on Simulation Methods in Tax Policy Analysis, Palm Beach, Florida, January 26–27, 1981; and Feldstein and Pellechio, "Social Security Wealth: The Impact of Alternative Inflation Adjustments," pp. 91–117.

15. To illustrate this point, assume that a man pays payroll taxes of $2,500 a year for forty years (including the employer tax) and receives the same real benefit as if he had invested that amount at 2 percent real interest. If the expected value of the resulting benefits equals the accumulated fund and is discounted at 3 percent real interest (rather than the actual return of 2 percent), he will appear to be receiving benefits worth $11,495 less in present value than the taxes he paid, although he is receiving a positive real return of 2 percent a year. This illustration ignores the risk of death before retirement.

securities could have yielded a portfolio that would have behaved as if it were indexed.[16] But there is no guarantee that this portfolio will continue to behave as if it were indexed. Furthermore, the real rate of return on such a portfolio was close to zero. Since investors revealed a willingness to purchase the assets entering this portfolio at prices that yielded a zero real rate of return, it is possible to argue that the market has indicated that it would accept indexed bonds with a zero real rate of return and that a zero discount rate should be used in evaluating social security benefits; by such a criterion, all cohorts now and for the foreseeable future would receive social security benefits worth far more than the taxes they pay.[17] Were government or private organizations to issue indexed bonds in large quantities, a market test would be made of the real rate of return that investors would require such securities to offer; pending such action, one can only speculate about the premium (in other words, the lower discount rate) investors would place on indexed securities and, by inference, on indexed social security benefits.

In addition to the valuation of one of social security's unique and, perhaps, most valuable characteristics, questions remain about what rate of return a pay-as-you-go social security system should be expected to yield and about the conditions under which the accumulation of social security reserves would yield additional benefits.

It has been shown that a pay-as-you-go social security system, one in which essentially no reserves are accumulated and perforce none can be invested, yields an implicit rate of return to covered workers on their tax payments that is equal to the sum of the rate of growth of the labor force and the rate of increase in wages.[18] This return arises from the simple fact that the flow of taxes from a work force that is growing larger

16. Zvi Bodie, "Investment Strategy in an Inflationary Environment," National Bureau of Economic Research Working Paper 701, June 1981.

17. Such an argument would be highly questionable, however, because it would involve the unwarranted assumption that the same "price" would be appropriate for social security benefits, which constitute a major component of the assets of most families and which are not sold on free markets, as is appropriate to a combination of assets that only sophisticated investors might have purchased.

18. Paul A. Samuelson, "An Exact Consumption-Loan Model of Interest with or without the Social Contrivance of Money," *Journal of Political Economy*, vol. 66 (December 1958), pp. 467–82; and Henry J. Aaron, "The Social Insurance Paradox," *Canadian Journal of Economics and Political Science*, vol. 32 (August 1966), pp. 371–77. This conclusion holds only if the ratio of the time spent in retirement to the time spent in the labor force is unchanged. If longevity increases, the rate of return rises unless the "retirement age" is deferred so that the ratio of working life to years in retirement is maintained.

and richer yields enough in revenues to finance benefits for the retired greater than the taxes they paid during their working years. If the labor force grows at, say, 1 percent a year and output per worker grows at, say, 1.5 percent a year, social security beneficiaries will receive benefits equal to those they would have received if they had invested at a 2.5 percent real rate of interest the taxes they previously paid. While these numbers are hypothetical and illustrative, the actual implicit rate, whatever it may be, provides a benchmark for a number of important choices.

First, and most important, if real investments yield a higher rate of return than this implicit, pay-as-you-go rate, there is a strong case for increasing real investments in the economy at large.[19] Resources are necessary to finance such real investment, and they can come from increased personal, business, or government saving. Additional government saving (or reduced dissaving) can be achieved by boosting taxes (perhaps including payroll taxes) or cutting spending (perhaps including social security benefits). The fact that investment opportunities exist in the economy does not indicate what mechanism should be selected to finance them. That choice hinges on such other political and economic considerations as the effect of the choice on the distribution of income or on the role of the government in economic activity.[20] In addition, even if the supply of saving constitutes the effective long-run constraint on investment, at any particular moment investment may be limited not by a shortage of saving but by a lack of investment. At such times an increase in saving may have little or no effect on investment. The point is that the existence of high real rates of return on investments does not imply anything about the financing of social security.

Nor does it carry any implications about whether individual workers are receiving their money's worth on their payroll taxes. That question

19. Robert M. Solow, "A Contribution to the Theory of Economic Growth," *Quarterly Journal of Economics,* vol. 70 (February 1956), pp. 65–94; and "Comment," *Review of Economic Studies,* vol. 39 (June 1962), pp. 255–57.

20. For example, some analysts have suggested that rather than increase payroll taxes to maintain benefits when the ratio of retirees to active workers increases, it would be desirable to increase taxes enough before the aged population increases to build up a trust fund sufficient to permit the same tax rate to be maintained from now on. Their motivation is a belief that the good fortune of working when there are relatively few retirees should not excuse the present generation from bearing part of the looming cost of supporting the baby boom when that generation retires. Although this argument is open to serious challenge, it explicitly brings to bear considerations of the distribution of income among generations on the question of how large the social security trust fund should be.

hinges on whether they could earn comparably secure and comparably high real rates of return through alternative investments available to them and on whether social security benefits are too high, too low, or about right. In answering this question, the fact that returns on the stock market, real estate, or some other asset may have been higher over some particular historical period is relevant, but hardly conclusive. Real rates of return on all private assets to which individuals and financial intermediaries have access have been extremely unstable during the twentieth century; and the experience of the 1970s drove home the fact that although these fluctuations may not now reach the catastrophic proportions typical of earlier decades, they have by no means disappeared.

What this all means is that simple calculations of the internal rate of return or of the present discounted value, though not without interest for certain purposes, miss most of the interesting and important questions about whether different cohorts of workers get their money's worth from social security and whether reserves should be accumulated. They place no value on the full protection against inflation that only social security now provides. In addition, the calculations do not address the fundamental question of the political, economic, and social value at the margin of social security benefits. Their use to justify one or another policy regarding the accumulation of reserves confuses a theorem of growth theory regarding the desirability of additional investment when the rate of return is greater than the sum of population and productivity growth with the means of achieving that end.

Effects within Cohorts

Such calculations are of great value, however, for examining the relative treatment of different groups because not all members of a given cohort are treated equally. Workers with low covered earnings receive more in benefits per dollar of earnings and taxes paid than do workers with high earnings. Similarly, couples receive more than do single persons with the same earnings. Thus some workers within a cohort that enjoys an internal rate of return of, say, 3 percent on the average will receive much higher and some much lower internal rates of return.

Friedman pointed out that inadvertent differences in rates of return may also occur.[21] Thus people who start working relatively late in life

21. The question of the relative treatment of different groups among which the Social Security Act draws no explicit distinction was raised by Milton Friedman in Wilbur Cohen and Milton Friedman, *Social Security: Universal or Selective?* (American Enterprise Institute for Public Policy Research, 1972).

tend to receive a higher rate of return than do workers who enter the labor force early, even if they have the same average earnings, because the late entrants pay taxes for a briefer period. Similarly, he argued that whites do better than blacks with the same earnings history because they have longer life expectancies. Friedman hypothesized that these and other factors offset or eliminate the putative progressivity of the social security benefit formula.

Okonkwo and I separately measured the degree to which such factors as life expectancy and age of entry might offset progressivity in the benefit formula.[22] Okonkwo reported that the average internal rate of return for blacks is higher than that for whites (because blacks earn less than nonblacks do), but is lower for blacks than for whites at the same earnings level (because blacks have lower life expectancies than do whites). I found that variation in the age of entry into the labor force has a large effect on the ratio of benefits to costs that could potentially completely offset the progressivity of the benefit formula, but that nonwhites nevertheless have a higher ratio of benefits to costs than do whites. Leimer incorporated longitudinal data on the actual ages of entry and schooling and on earnings of workers with different levels of education and found these factors insufficient to offset the progressivity of the benefit formula.[23]

All these analyses made a number of simplifying assumptions, some of which biased their results. For example, I assumed that all workers start receiving full benefits at age sixty-five; in fact, the earnings test is more likely to reduce the benefits of high earners than of the low ones.[24] Furthermore, both Okonkwo and I based our studies on synthetic earnings profiles of supposedly representative workers.

These and other shortcomings were remedied by Freiden and others in a study based on actual earnings histories drawn from social security records.[25] They concluded that the direction of the effects of age of entry

22. Ubadigbo Okonkwo, "Individual Equity Under Social Security: Some Black-White Comparisons," a paper prepared for the Eighty-sixth Annual Meeting of the American Economic Association, New York, December 28, 1973; and Henry J. Aaron, with the assistance of Philip Spevak, "Demographic Effects on the Equity of Social Security Benefits," in Martin S. Feldstein and Robert P. Inman, eds., *The Economics of Public Services* (London: Macmillan, 1977), pp. 151–73.

23. Dean R. Leimer, "Projected Rates of Return to Future Social Security Retirees under Alternative Benefit Structures," *Policy Analysis with Social Security Research Files,* Research Report 52, pp. 235–67.

24. A. B. Atkinson, "Discussion," in Feldstein and Inman, eds., *The Economics of Public Services,* p. 477.

25. Freiden, Leimer, and Hoffman, *Internal Rates of Return to Retired Worker-Only Beneficiaries under Social Security, 1967–1970.*

and life expectancy were as hypothesized by Friedman, but weaker than I estimated. They also found that the internal rate of return for black men and women was significantly higher than that for their white counterparts.[26]

None of these studies adequately took into account survivor or disability insurance benefits. These benefits disproportionately accrue to nonwhites, precisely because of the higher mortality and disability rates that reduce the proportion of nonwhite old age insurance beneficiaries.[27]

On balance, it is clear that such factors as differential mortality and age of entry offset, but do not eliminate, the progressivity of the social security benefit formula, that survivors and disability insurance reinforce it, and that social security has provided relatively larger lifetime wealth increments to cohorts with low earnings and, within those cohorts, to workers with low earnings.

Indirect Distributional Effects

The effects of social security on the distribution of income described in this chapter arise directly from payroll taxes and social security benefits. In addition, however, social security has the potential to change the distribution of income indirectly. To the extent that social security alters the supply of labor or the size of the capital stock, it can change real wage rates or the rate of return on capital. In principle, these effects can be large. Feldstein, for example, calculated that social security had reduced the capital stock by enough to reduce real wages significantly and to boost the real rate of return to owners of capital; but, as noted above, his underlying estimates proved to be faulty. Zeckhauser has shown that changes in factor supplies in response to various taxes can produce large and surprising distributional effects of the kind here characterized as secondary.[28]

---

26. The internal rates of return to all white men and women were 11.46 percent and 17.03 percent, respectively, for the cohorts reaching retirement age from 1967 to 1970; for nonwhite men and women the rates were 13.39 percent and 22.45 percent, respectively, in the same years. See Freiden, Leimer, and Hoffman, pp. 43–48.

27. See *Report of the 1979 Advisory Council on Social Security*, pp. 125–38.

28. Richard Zeckhauser, "Taxes in Fantasy, or Most Any Tax on Labor Can Turn Out to Help the Laborers," *Journal of Public Economics,* vol. 8 (October 1977), pp. 133–50.

The absence of reliable estimates of the effects of social security on factor supplies renders any estimates of the size of such secondary distributional effects purely speculative. Although it is important to keep these secondary effects in mind and to recognize that they may be very important, there is little that can be said about them in the current state of empirical confusion.

CHAPTER SEVEN

Conclusion

THE social security system affects people throughout their lives, at work and in retirement. Although it plays a large part in American society, its effects on saving and labor supply are hard to measure. The theoretical effects of even simple annuities are difficult to unravel. But social security is much more than a simple annuity. Achieving a theoretical consensus on how so complex a system should influence behavior has proven elusive. Theorists have developed alternative analytical frameworks for looking at the effects of social security. But all involve extreme assumptions introduced to ensure analytical tractability, and each seems to describe the behavior of some, but not all or even most people. The reasonable position for the policymaker or ordinary citizen to take is that no single model is generally applicable. The shortcomings of available data have created additional roadblocks to measuring the effects of the social security system on economic behavior. My own view is that empirical research eventually will validate the modified short-horizon model as the most useful framework for thinking about the effects of social security on economic behavior; but that is merely a prediction.

For all these reasons the analyst can provide relatively little good evidence to the policymaker who is trying to decide whether and how to alter the social security system regarding the effects that social security has had on economic behavior. The direct primary effects of social security on the distribution of income in any year are large because social security moves disposable income from relatively high income, active workers to the relatively low-income retired, disabled, and survivors. Much of this annual redistribution is a repayment of past taxes and hence is not redistributive within the life-cycle context. But a large part today is a redistribution from future, relatively high-income cohorts to relatively low-income cohorts of present and past retirees. Lack of evidence on the effects of social security on saving and labor supply translates into a lack of evidence about the secondary effects of social security on factor incomes.

If policymakers cannot rely on clear evidence of the effects of social security to guide their deliberations, they will have to turn to a broader and more diffuse consideration of the role that a mandatory social insurance system should play in a modern industrial society. Even a cursory survey of the social insurance systems of other industrial countries will reveal the diversity of the institutions that various nations have erected to deal with a shared problem of how to ensure a basic income for people who are retired, disabled, widowed, or orphaned. Their experience dramatizes that arrangements other than the particular ones adopted by the United States can achieve this goal.

Such a survey will also reveal that other nations are now experiencing demographic problems as serious as those the United States will encounter in the next century and that those nations now have social insurance systems as generous as that in the United States. It will also show that the total tax burdens of most of these nations exceed that of the United States, even if one includes national defense and state and local expenditures. There can be no doubt that the United States is rich enough to sustain social security cash benefits for the indefinite future. (There is far more doubt that it can sustain the system of financing health care, in general, or medicare hospital insurance, in particular; but that issue is outside the scope of this book.)

As the president, Congress, and the American people continue the difficult task of deciding how to deal with the short-run financial problems of the social security system and of considering whether and how to modify the system over the long run, they should not encumber an already difficult political task with economic myth. There is no evidence about the economic effects of social behavior sufficiently strong to justify significant changes in the fundamental retirement income system of the nation. And other nations have proven able to sustain social insurance systems at least as generous as that of the United States with aged populations as large as America's will be during the next century. Strong cases based on equity can be made for changes in the structure of social security benefits; for example, the payment to one-earner families of benefits larger than those paid to two-earner families with the same earned income is an anachronism that should be ended.[1]

1. Two-earner families receive extra disability and survivor protection beyond that available to one-earner families. In addition, one- and two-earner families with the same

Fundamental changes, however, must rest on political considerations. The possibility that the economy will continue to grow slowly suggests that commitments to rising government expenditures should be reexamined. For example, the present benefit formula automatically alters the formula used for computing initial retirement benefits to provide retirees with the benefits of rising productivity, as well as to offset the effects of inflation.[2] I believe that the responsibility for deciding whether benefits should be increased faster than prices should be left to successive Congresses, so that they can decide on the distribution of such gains—among retirees, other beneficiaries of public services, or taxpayers. For this reason, a decision to alter the formula used for computing initial benefits so that not all the gains from rising productivity were automatically distributed would have certain desirable features.[3] And it would improve the capacity of the political process to respond to the many problems that would arise if the future economic performance of the United States continues to be poor. But neither this proposal nor the many others now under discussion should be approved or disapproved on the basis that anyone has established with any certainty the economic effects of the current system or of the alternatives or because of a fear that Americans cannot afford the system they have.

---

earned income do not have equal economic circumstances. These factors justify somewhat smaller retirement benefits for two-earner families than for one-earner families with the same total earnings, but not the large differences that result under current law.

2. After this initial computation, benefits are then adjusted only for inflation.

3. See Henry J. Aaron and others, *Report of the 1979 Advisory Council on Social Security* (GPO, 1980), pp. 212–15.